Better Bible Teaching for Intermediates

BETTER
BIBLE TEACHING
FOR
INTERMEDIATES

Annie Ward Byrd

Convention Press

NASHVILLE　　　　　TENNESSEE

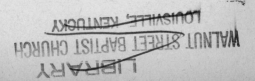

© 1959 • Convention Press

Nashville, Tennessee
All right reserved
International copyright secured

5117-52

Code Number: Church Study Course

This book is number 1752 in
category 17, section for
Adults and Young People.

Library of Congress Catalog Card Number: 59–9968
Printed in the United States of America
5. AT 65 R.R.D.

DEDICATED TO THE TEENS
I HAVE TAUGHT

About the Author

ANNIE WARD BYRD was born and reared in Mississippi. She is the daughter of a former state Sunday school secretary.

She graduated as valedictorian of her class at senior high school and with honors from Mississippi Woman's College. Later she did graduate study in English at the University of North Carolina and at Tulane University. She received the Master of Arts degree at George Peabody College, with major in sociology and minor in education.

Miss Byrd taught English in high school in Drew, Mississippi, and later became principal of the same high school. During her career at Drew, she was active as sponsor and adviser for extra-curricular youth activities.

She came to the Sunday School Board in 1940, as editor of Intermediate Sunday school lesson materials (Graded and Uniform). She is a member of the Committee on the Uniform Lesson Series of the National Council; a worker in Intermediate II department of First Baptist Church, Nashville, Tennessee; and the author of a book of program materials, *Youth at Worship*.

In November, 1961, Miss Byrd gave up her work as editor to become editorial co-ordinator for the Education Division of the Baptist Sunday School Board.

In 1962 she was awarded a Doctor of Literature degree by William Carey College, Hattiesburg, Mississippi.

Contents

Church Study Course

THE CHURCH STUDY COURSE began October 1, 1959. It is a merger of three courses previously promoted by the Sunday School Board —the Sunday School Training Course, the Graded Training Union Study Course, and the Church Music Training Course. On October 1, 1961, the Woman's Missionary Union principles and methods studies were added.

The course is fully graded. The system of awards provides a series of five diplomas of twenty books each for Adults or Young People, two diplomas of five books each for Intermediates, and two diplomas of five books each for Juniors.

The course is comprehensive, with books grouped into twenty categories. The purpose of the course is to help Christians to grow in knowledge and conviction, to help them to grow toward maturity in Christian character and competence for service, to encourage them to participate worthily as workers in their churches, and to develop leaders for all phases of church life and work.

The Church Study Course is promoted by the Baptist Sunday School Board, 127 Ninth Avenue, North, Nashville, Tennessee 37203, through its Sunday School, Training Union, Church Music, and Church Administration departments; by the Woman's Missionary Union, 600 North Twentieth Street, Birmingham, Alabama 35203; and by the respective departments in the states affiliated with the Southern Baptist Convention. A description of the course and the system of awards may be found in the leaflet "Trained Workmen," which may be obtained without charge from any one of these departments.

A record of all awards earned should be maintained in each church. A person should be designated by the church to keep the files. Forms for such records may be ordered from any Baptist Book Store.

Requirements for Credit in Class
or Home Study

IF CREDIT IS DESIRED for the study of this book in a class or by home study, the following requirements must be met:

I. IN CLASSWORK

1. The class must meet a minimum of seven and one-half clock hours. The required time does not include assembly periods. Ten class periods of forty-five minutes each are recommended. (If laboratory or clinical work is desired in specialized or technical courses, this requirement may be met by six clock hours of classwork and three clock hours of supervised laboratory or clinical work.)

2. A class member who attends all class sessions and completes the reading of the book within a week following the last class session will not be required to do any written work for credit.

3. A class member who is absent from one or more sessions must answer the questions (pp. 129-131) on all chapters he misses. In such a case, he must turn in his paper within a week, and he must certify that he has read the book.

4. The teacher should request an award for himself. A person who teaches a book in the section for Intermediates or Juniors (any category) or conducts an approved unit of instruction for Nursery, Beginner, or Primary children will be granted an award in category 11, Special Studies, which will count as an elective on his own diploma. He should specify in his request the name of the book taught, or the unit conducted for Nursery, Beginner, or Primary children.

5. The teacher should complete the "Request for Book Awards —Class Study" (Form 150) and forward it within two weeks after the completion of the class to the Church Study Course Awards Office, 127 Ninth Avenue, North, Nashville, Tennessee 37203.

II. IN HOME STUDY

1. A person who does not attend any class session may receive credit by answering all questions for written work as indicated in the book (pp. 129-131). When a person turns in his paper on home study, he must certify that he has read the book.

2. Students may find profit in studying the text together, but individual papers are required. Carbon copies or duplicates in any form cannot be accepted.

3. Home study work papers may be graded by the pastor or a person designated by him, or they may be sent to the Church Study Course Awards Office for grading. The form entitled "Request for Book Awards—Home Study" (Form 151) must be used in requesting awards. It should be mailed to Church Study Course Awards Office, 127 Ninth Avenue, North, Nashville, Tennessee 37203.

III. CREDIT FOR THIS BOOK

This book is number 1752 in category 17, section for Adults and Young People.

CHAPTER 1

I. A BASIC UNDERSTANDING NEEDED
   1. Teaching Is Not—
   2. Teaching Is—

II. OUR OBJECTIVES CONSIDERED
   1. Conversion
   2. Church Membership
   3. Worship
   4. Christian Knowledge and Conviction
   5. Christian Attitudes and Appreciations
   6. Christian Living
   7. Service

III. A CREATIVE APPROACH DESIRED

1

Teaching, a Dangerous Opportunity

MANY OF YOU, my brothers, should avoid becoming teachers."
Are you surprised to know that James, the half brother of our
Lord, wrote this warning to first-century Christians? If he
were writing to twentieth-century Christians, he would
doubtless say the same thing for the same reason: "You know
that we teachers are going to be judged with stricter judgment than other people" (James 3:1 Williams' translation).[1]

Teaching is very serious business. Why? Anyone who at-
tempts to bring about change in another or to direct the
changes taking place in the life of another assumes a dangerous responsibility. On the other hand, the person who fails
to try to bring about changes of the right sort or to direct
change to a good end passes up a glorious opportunity.

This book is designed to help teachers and potential workers with youth know better how to effect and direct changes
in their pupils so that teen-agers today may increase "in
wisdom and stature, and in favour with God and man."

I. A BASIC UNDERSTANDING NEEDED

At the outset we (readers and author) need to agree upon
the meaning of the term "teaching."

Some words are hard to define because they are so inclu-
sive. Probably no cut-and-dried, dictionary-type definition
of teaching would ever be completely satisfactory. A basic
idea of what is included, or just a "working definition," can
serve a better purpose. Let us see whether we can develop
such a working concept.

1

1. *Teaching Is Not—*

A negative approach is one way of clarifying a term. Let's note some activities that are similar to teaching but are not actual teaching situations.

(1) *Telling.*—There was a time when in a book of this type teaching might have been defined as the act of "imparting knowledge"—as if information could be handed out by the teacher in packaged form. That time has passed, however, for research in the area of teaching and learning verifies the fact that something has to happen on the inside of a person before he really learns or before the teacher has really taught.

Though telling may be one medium of teaching (as in a lecture, for instance), teaching itself involves a great deal more than the oral transmission of information from teacher to pupil.

(2) *Preaching.*—Likely there is an element of teaching in almost all sermons one hears, but preaching and teaching are distinct ministries. Preaching is one-way communication. Attitudes may be changed and decisions may be made as an outgrowth of the pastor's exhortations. A Sunday school teacher should not think for a minute, however, that he would be justified in using the preaching technique in a class of seven or eight teen-age boys. Each activity has a significant place, but the process of teaching is not to be confused with the act of preaching.

(3) *Showing.*—Effective demonstration will contribute to the learning process. However, a pupil may watch his teacher perform a certain skill without acquiring that skill himself. The teacher who limits his activity to "showing," not getting any response from the pupil himself, will fall far short of his goal. To develop skills, even in the area of Christian living, requires "doing."

2. *Teaching Is—*

What, then, is teaching? The following analysis should lead to a working definition.

(1) *A process.*—Something happens when learning takes place. Teaching and learning are both dynamic, not static. The teacher challenges, and the pupil responds by translating ideas and facts into a form which he can use.

> Teaching is not like inducing a chemical reaction: it is much more like painting a picture or making a piece of music, or on a lower level like planting a garden or like writing a friendly letter.[2]

(2) *A co-operative process.*—Without learners there would be no teachers. Before teaching takes place, there must be response to the challenge issued by the teacher. The pupil has to "remake" for himself the facts or ideas which the teacher has helped him to discover. There is a flow from the stimulus of the teacher to awareness on the part of the pupil.

Another Person becomes a part of the co-operative process of teaching God's Word. The Holy Spirit works through the teacher to help the pupil become aware of his need and to realize how facts and ideas may be used to meet that need. A noted religious educator described the work of a Sunday school teacher as being this: "To bring individuals into the vicinity where God himself may speak through the Bible." Co-operating with God to make his Word meaningful is the teacher's mission.

(3) *A process resulting in change.*—Through the leadership of the Holy Spirit, action on the part of the teacher who really teaches will lead to reaction on the part of pupils. In other words, pupils will change when they are taught effectively.

"Conversion" is another word for change. And it suggests

to us in the field of Christian education the most significant change that can ever occur in the life of an individual, namely, the act of becoming a child of God through repentance from sin and through personal faith in Christ as Saviour and Lord. But the word "change" also includes growth as well as the initial conversion experience.

Let's formulate a statement summarizing the basic ideas incorporated thus far in the term "teaching," meaning in this instance Sunday school teaching. Consider this one: *Teaching is a co-operative enterprise of pupil, teacher, and the Holy Spirit, resulting in conversion and growth.*

II. OUR OBJECTIVES CONSIDERED

Frequent references will be made later to the fact that pupils should have a part in setting up their learning goals. One is naturally more interested in striving to reach objectives that are meaningful to him as an individual. Purposes must "make sense" to the learner; they must lead to the fulfilment of something he wants or needs, else he will not be motivated to try to achieve the goal.

But sometimes very significant needs are not felt, or at least not identified or recognized, even by adults, much less by Intermediates, who are still in the process of growing up. For that reason a basic list of age group objectives in the area of Christian teaching and training has been compiled by age-group workers at the Sunday School Board to be used as resource material. These are long-range aims, which must be broken down into specific learning goals related to pupil interests and needs. All church-related activities will help young people work toward the achievement of these goals: the Sunday school, Intermediate union, youth choir, GA's and RA's, for instance. Certainly the home and the public school will help, too. But the Sunday school must bear a major responsibility for leading teen-agers to let the living Christ take hold of their lives.

So teachers of Intermediates should have in mind always the seven great areas of spiritual need outlined in the discussion which follows.

These objectives are grounded in theology because teaching that is truly Christian must be rooted in biblical theology. There is a difference between character education and Christian teaching. Though our objectives include character education, our purpose goes beyond it, for we try to lead our pupils to put themselves unconditionally under the control of God's Spirit. Christian objectives for Intermediates include—

1. *Conversion*

If you were asked to name the one major objective of Bible teaching, doubtless you would say something like this: *to lead each unsaved Intermediate to experience the forgiving, saving grace of God through Jesus Christ.* Your answer would be correct.

But before he will turn to Christ, trusting him for salvation, the individual must first realize his failure to live up to God's standard of righteousness and his consequent need of a Saviour. Teachers must help bring about this realization.

2. *Church Membership*

Conversion should be just the beginning. Following that experience, the new Christian should be *guided into intelligent, active, and devoted membership in a New Testament church.* Our responsibility will be to lead him—

(1) To unite with a church by baptism upon his public profession of faith

(2) To grow in understanding and appreciation of the purposes, practices, and leadership of his church

(3) To grow in loyalty by attending services regularly and participating in the church program as a means of serving Christ and his fellow men

(4) To give faithfully and proportionately for the support of his church

3. *Worship*

If the young Christian is to grow, he must be *helped to make Christian worship a vital and constant part of his expanding experience.*

He needs to read his Bible daily in a spirit of devotion and to pray, to worship with his family, and to worship with the church fellowship of which he is a part.

4. *Christian Knowledge and Conviction*

Teachers have the opportunity *to help each Intermediate grow in biblical and Christian knowledge and conviction.*

(1) With respect to the Bible and the great realities of the Christian faith:

a. To develop a growing love for the Bible

b. To accept the Bible as a way by which God speaks to him and as the final authority in all matters of faith and conduct

c. To understand something of the origin of the Bible and of God's use of man in preparing and preserving it

d. To grow in understanding and mastery of biblical content, including customs, geography, history, and the great realities of the Christian faith

e. To acquire a growing comprehension of the meaning of the Christian faith and of how these Bible truths apply to personal daily living and to community and world problems

f. To commit choice Bible passages to memory

(2) With respect to the Christian movement and to his church and denomination:

A Christian teen-ager should learn some outstanding facts of Christian history and should grow in understanding of the distinctive features of Baptist history, doctrine, and polity and of the organization, program, problems, and needs of Southern Baptists.

5. *Christian Attitudes and Appreciations*

Our aim in this area is *to help the pupil develop Christian attitudes and appreciations in every area of his experience.*

(1) *Regarding God.*—As the teen-ager develops in his concept of God, his love for the Heavenly Father and Jesus as Saviour and Lord will grow deeper. That deepening appreciation will be revealed through his reverence for God and his laws, through dependence upon the Holy Spirit for guidance, and through a sense of gratitude for all of God's goodness.

(2) *Regarding the meaning of existence.*—The Intermediate will grow in his realization that all existence is an expression of God's goodness, wisdom, and power. He will realize that every person, because he is created in the image of God, is of infinite worth, has marvelous possibilities, and possesses spiritual need which only God can supply.

(3) *Regarding self.*—The Intermediate needs to appreciate his body and mind as gifts from God, which should be cared for, developed, and used for God's glory and the good of others. His personal ideal should be the attainment of a mature Christian personality.

(4) *Regarding others.*—The young Christian should accept the responsibility for his influence upon others, should develop an attitude of unselfish devotion to the welfare of people of all cultures, races, and social levels, and should feel sincere concern for the salvation of others.

(5) *Regarding divine institutions.*—Teachers should help their pupils recognize that the Lord's Day, the ordinances of baptism and the Lord's Supper, and the institution of marriage and family life should be used to honor Christ. They need also to respect civil government and to assume the responsibilities of good citizenship.

6. *Christian Living*

In order to attain mature Christian stature, pupils need guidance *in learning skills and in developing habits which promote personal growth and Christian conduct.* Accepting the Bible and the Holy Spirit as guides, understanding why and how to pray, and seeking to pattern all personal conduct in accordance with the teachings, spirit, and example of Jesus will promote such growth.

7. *Service*

If our pupils are to become active Christian disciples, we must help them *to develop skill in Christian service.* This means helping each Intermediate—

(1) To witness loyally to his Christian faith and to seek to win others to Jesus Christ

(2) To seek God's will for his life and to prepare for a vocation in keeping with that will

(3) To appreciate and take advantage of the training and service opportunities offered him in his church program

(4) To give faithfully of his money from worthy motives and according to biblical teaching for the support of his church and the spread of the gospel throughout the world

(5) To do deeds of helpfulness as a habit in daily life

III. A Creative Approach Desired

Are you discouraged by the above list of objectives toward which you and your pupils must strive? You should not be! Instead, make up your mind that with the help of God, you are going to develop as a Christian teacher and are going to help your class grow in Christlikeness. The following excerpt should stimulate you to fulfil your resolution:

> The question that inevitably comes to mind is whether or not we who work in religion (or in whom religion works) are in our field as creative as scientists are in theirs. For instance,

do we bring the same intensity of imaginative thought to understanding the things of God that the men at Redstone Arsenal are giving to rockets? Is the Kingdom of Christ as intriguing as the Kingdom of Space? Does it call for us the same dedication as it takes to place a satellite into orbit?

The Christian who uses his imagination creatively is a person of high adventure. He dares to believe that there is a world of unseen spiritual reality that is as real as that which his senses report. Men of this kind are the Abrahams who look up into the stars and claim a new nation, generations before it is born. They are the Moseses who hear God speak in bushes that burn and are not consumed. They are like the Christ who for the joy that was set before him endured the cross.

These persons of creativity are the dreamers and the workers too. Out of the imperfections of the present they build a more perfect day that is to come. And when it is delayed, when war and selfishness set back its pace, they keep on believing. They are the engineers of the Kingdom of God who follow blueprints not of their own making, but of God's. Such persons never give up hoping for the bright new world.[3]

FOR FURTHER CONSIDERATION

1. Recall an instance from your youth when you really learned something (not necessarily in school). Analyze the experience enough to identify the stimulus, the teacher, and the outcome.
2. Why isn't character education for youth a sufficiently worthy goal for the Sunday school ministry?
3. What is your idea of the difference between long-range aims and specific learning goals? Illustrate by using one of the seven major areas outlined in this chapter.
4. Why is it important for Sunday school teachers to be *dreamers* as well as *workers*?
5. With which should Sunday school be more vitally concerned: what a pupil knows or what a pupil is?

[1] Charles W. Williams, *The New Testament in the Language of the People* (Chicago: Moody Press, 1955). Used by permission.

[2] Gilbert Highet, *The Art of Teaching* (New York: Vintage Books, 1956), p. viii. Used by permission of Alfred A. Knopf, Inc.

[3] Charles M. Layman, "On Being Creative," *International Journal of Religious Education,* June, 1958, p. 3. Used by permission.

CHAPTER 2

I. TEEN-AGERS RESPOND TO TEACHERS WHO—

1. Understand and Encourage Them
2. Create Friendly Atmosphere in the Classroom
3. Stimulate Pupil Participation
4. Relate Content to Felt Needs of Pupils
5. Know More Than Pupils Know
6. Are Enthusiastic About the Subject and About Teaching
7. Can Explain Clearly and Thoroughly
8. Deserve Respect of Pupils
9. Are Firm but Fair

II. A SUNDAY SCHOOL TEACHER NEEDS—

1. To Be Dedicated to His Task
2. To Know His Pupils
3. To Make Thorough Preparation
4. To Understand Teaching-Learning Principles
5. To Use Good Teaching Techniques
6. To Lead an Exemplary Life

2

The Teacher, Creator of Opportunities

THINK BACK over your teen years in school. Whom do you remember to have been your best teacher? Why do you remember that particular person especially?

> [The ideal teacher] guides his students, but does not pull them along; he urges them to go forward and does not suppress them; he opens the way, but does not take them to the place. Guiding without pulling makes the process of learning gentle; urging without suppressing makes the process of learning easy; and opening the way without leading the students to the place makes them think for themselves.[1]

This portrait painted in words by a renowned, ancient, pagan teacher has a significant message for the present-day Christian teacher who will take time to study the philosophy revealed in these two sentences.

After the brief preview in chapter 1 of the meaning of the term teaching and of the objectives of Christian teaching, the next step is to consider how to become the kind of teacher to do the kind of job needed. This discussion should evoke sincere, objective soul-searching on the part of every teacher.

I. TEEN-AGERS RESPOND TO TEACHERS WHO—

Since we are primarily concerned about doing a better job of working with Intermediates, we should listen to the young people themselves in order to know the qualities their "ideal" teachers have. The following list is an almost verbatim report of what some fifteen- and sixteen-year-old Intermediates had to say about teachers they consider good. They praised those who—

1. *Understand and Encourage Them*

Youngsters can detect intuitively whether they are liked and are respected and accepted. Naturally, they respond to a person who is able and willing to see their point of view. They would not have liked a university professor who remarked one day, while observing some cute teen-age girls waiting to be seated in a public tearoom: "Girls that age ought to be locked up until they get to be college freshmen, at least. I don't see how anybody ever puts up with them!"

When trouble arises between a teen-ager and an adult, whether parent or teacher, the youngster invariably feels that he *is not understood.*

Because they are living through a transitional stage, Intermediates many times become discouraged or even despondent. They need the encouragement and confidence of an understanding adult. This tribute paid to public school teachers by a former gypsy girl, now a leader in the field of religious education in her own denomination, expresses this idea quite effectively:

> That was what made me love teachers. They believed in me. They seemed to expect good things from me. The local children shunned me because I was a dirty gypsy. The camper kids called me smarty and stuck-up because I liked school and would not dip snuff or chew on cigarette butts. Even my parents mocked me, ridiculed my "highfalutin ways" and laughed at me for "trying to be like those nasty nice schoolteachers." But the teachers seemed to know me as I was. They could see the spirit flickering dimly within that tattered caricature of childhood. They cared enough to fan the trembling flame.[2]

If ever we are to help our pupils grow in spiritual stature, we must accept them as they are and must "care enough to fan the trembling flame."

2. *Create Friendly Atmosphere in the Classroom*

High on the list of favorite teacher qualities is this one: friendliness in the classroom. Since the attitude of the teacher is contagious, he is the key to the spirit of the entire class.

If he is cold and indifferent, pupils will find it hard, if not impossible, to be friendly and sympathetic with each other. Warmth is needed for germinating ideas in teen-age minds just as it is needed for germinating seed in a flower bed. Precepts about kindness and love will fall on deaf ears if teachers aren't able to demonstrate these qualities in the classroom.

3. *Stimulate Pupil Participation*

Favorite teachers do not do all the talking! Instead, they abide by the slogan, "Talk less, and teach more."

One thirteen-year-old expressed his feeling in these strong words:

> I dislike teachers who bore students with lengthy notes, and will yell at the slightest little thing. I *hate* teachers who don't let you say one single word. I *double hate* teachers who pick on one person all the time. I don't like a teacher who will not reason out, as in math; a person who will not let you tell the way you used to work a problem.[3]

In the book *Everybody's Business—Our Children,* Mauree Applegate tells of the mother who took her son to an ear specialist because the child paid no attention when she talked. In response to the doctor's question as to whether he had trouble hearing, the boy replied that he did not have trouble hearing—he had trouble *listening!*

Psychologists confirm the fact that pupils do not learn easily by listening to instruction. So there is a psychological basis for liking a teacher who builds his lessons around pupil reaction and response. Other chapters in this book will discuss how teachers may lead pupils to participate meaningfully during the class period; it is important to know now that participation is essential if teaching is to be effective.

4. *Relate Content to Felt Needs of Pupils*

The Sunday school lesson was based on the ministry of John the Baptist, including the baptism of Jesus. As he left the classroom, one fellow remarked: "The teacher explained the difference between John's baptism and Jesus' baptism clearly enough, I suppose. But what I wanted to know is the difference between the Methodist idea of baptism and Baptist beliefs about it."

Apparently the teacher had taught a lesson without sensing or finding out what his pupils really wanted to know in relation to the subject. The teacher may have felt that he had taught a good lesson, but the class members weren't satisfied for they had not learned what they needed to know.

Content, even biblical content, is not an end in itself. John wrote, you recall, for this purpose: "These are written, that ye might believe that Jesus is the Christ, the Son of God; and that believing ye might have life through his name" (John 20:31). In order to appropriate content, in order to make it their own, pupils must feel that it is relevant to them personally.

5. *Know More Than Pupils Know*

Have you ever been in a class where you felt that the teacher was barely a page ahead of his pupils? Had you asked a question based on the next chapter, he would have been quite disconcerted.

Junior and senior high school students do not expect their teachers to know everything. (Elementary pupils probably think theirs do!) But they do respect the teacher whose horizons are broad and whose thoughts are deep. They have "genuine respect for the teacher who can serve an ample intellectual fare"! [4]

"One cannot understand the rudiments of an important subject without knowing its higher levels—at least, not well enough to teach it." [5] A child may be able to recite the multiplication tables or to add simple sums, but that limited knowledge does not qualify him to teach arithmetic to others. A teacher must have a great reservoir of knowledge to draw upon and be constantly adding to his knowledge through further study.

6. Are Enthusiastic About the Subject and About Teaching

Why do some students dread a unit of lessons in the Old Testament? Because some teachers dread teaching Old Testament lessons. Intermediates see through their teachers rather easily. If the teacher isn't enthusiastic over the lesson, the pupil will figure that it isn't worth learning, anyway.

Pity the class whose teacher doesn't really like to teach but has accepted the job because he felt it his duty to do so or because the pastor or superintendent talked him into doing it or because he was bored sitting in a class taught by someone else. Nothing thrilling or stimulating will happen in one of his classes.

7. Can Explain Clearly and Thoroughly

Teaching is a great deal more than telling or trying "to get ideas across." But there comes a time, probably in nearly every lesson, when the teacher needs to clarify a statement or a situation. The person who cannot communicate with his pupils feels inadequate and leaves his students confused and frustrated. The ability to explain in such a way that another is helped to see is a gift to be cultivated.

8. Deserve Respect of Pupils

Older Intermediates tend to be realistic and objective in

their judgments. They are often more tolerant in judging other people than adults are. For that reason they quickly reject a teacher who tries to put something over on them.

The teener, who likes to reason and argue and pick up an error in a discussion, is quick to detect pretense and weaknesses in his teacher, whether weakness in character or in skill. A wholesome relationship between teacher and pupil must grow out of mutual respect.

9. *Are Firm but Fair*

Though teen-age pupils will often "go just as far" as a teacher will let them, in the end they respect the teacher who keeps the classroom situation well in hand. This statement by an eminent adolescent psychologist has significance for the Sunday school teacher of Intermediates as well as for a secular school teacher:

> There are findings supporting the idea that democratic procedures promote a child's development better than autocratic procedures. But whatever the findings on this score may be, many adults have been uncertain about what it means to be democratic or permissive. Some seem to have assumed that they should swing from one extreme to another; if their upbringing was strict they should now be lenient; if their education was "hard," they should be "soft"; if they were closely supervised and restrained as children their proper policy should be to allow children unlimited freedom.
>
> Actually, of course, to allow a child (or the adolescent about whom we now are concerned) unlimited freedom in the name of being democratic is to foster chaos. No young person has within himself the wisdom, judgment, and ability to make good use of unlimited freedom even if, in theory, it were possible to provide unlimited freedom.[6]

All youngsters want teachers (and parents) to be consistent in discipline, and certainly they want fairness in discipline. (Do you remember the "double hate" of the thirteen-year-old quoted earlier?)

Some teachers need to realize that a sense of humor is an aid, not a hindrance, to classroom discipline. So is a relaxed, friendly attitude. In fact, the teen-agers who compiled this list of desirable qualities said, "The kind of teacher we're talking about doesn't have to worry about discipline. It will take care of itself."

II. A SUNDAY SCHOOL TEACHER NEEDS—

Since a teacher's role is so important in the development of teen-age boys and girls, the Sunday school teacher should be especially concerned about his responsibility. Let's consider how he can use the information as to what adolescents want in a teacher and how he can use his role as teacher to help youngsters achieve the objectives of Christian education outlined in the preceding chapter.

1. *To Be Dedicated to His Task*

In the first place, the teacher must feel that he is where God wants him to be, doing what God wants him to do. He must believe with all his heart that teaching a Sunday school class of teen-agers is important and that it is worthy of the best effort of the most capable, most deeply consecrated person.

Sometimes people who do not feel that they know enough or are good enough to teach adults accept an Intermediate class without hesitation. All the evidence points to the fact that young folk are so much more likely to change than adults that teaching them is an even more dangerous opportunity than teaching adults. Every teacher of teen-agers should feel that he is engaged in the most wonderful task of all (Of course, teachers of other age groups should feel the same way!) and that working in an Intermediate department week after week is a worthy way to serve the Lord.

The teacher will not be dedicated to his task unless his own faith is vital. He must know Christ as his personal

Saviour and Lord before he can lead another to know Christ, or even want to know him. The Bible must be to the teacher the living Word before he can make it live for his pupils. Before he will become an effective witness, he must believe that any person having reached the age of accountability without feeling a sense of guilt and need of the Saviour is lost and that personal faith in Christ is the only remedy for his sin.

Let us be assured that the personal faith of a teacher is a significant influence in the learning experience of his pupils and that the teacher's attitude toward his task will be reflected in the response of his pupils. That is why every Sunday school teacher should feel a genuine sense of dedication to his task.

2. *To Know His Pupils*

Real teaching can take place only when pupil and teacher understand each other and are working together to achieve a certain learning goal. How, then, does a teacher acquire a basic understanding of his pupils? There are many areas to be explored in an effort to know class members.

(1) Reading books and articles on adolescent psychology and on teen-age life is helpful in understanding individuals, as well as a group. Though no two people are exactly alike (there is no typical teen-ager), certain actions and reactions are characteristic of youngsters in the adolescent span of growth. In the next chapter some recent findings of outstanding adolescent psychologists are included because people trained in this field have valuable information to share with those of us who are particularly interested in the spiritual development of teen-agers.

Church libraries, as well as public libraries, provide reading material of this nature. From time to time, articles in *The Sunday School Builder* and the teacher books deal with Intermediate characteristics. Current magazines often carry excellent articles which Sunday school teachers will find helpful even though they are written from a secular point of view. Books which adolescents themselves like are an excellent resource for adults who are trying to understand them.

(2) Direct contact with pupils is a better resource, however, than just reading about them. For this reason Sunday school teachers must visit in the homes. Visits will reveal a great deal about a youngster's relationship with his parents, with other members of his family, and with friends his own age. The teacher can learn through conversation with the parents their attitude toward the church, the Sunday school, and toward spiritual matters in general. Parents can also share with teachers observable needs and interests of their child.

Teachers should invite pupils into their homes, too. Observing an Intermediate as he participates in extracurricular activities at school and in church services and organizational programs can be a revealing experience. Genuine interest on a teacher's part in a high school football team or in a dramatic production or in a student government project may open up a channel of communication between pupil and teacher that could never be opened during the thirty-five- or forty-minute period in the classroom on Sunday morning.

(3) Prayer and thoughtful meditation can help one gain insight into people as well as into passages of Scripture. A teacher should pray for an understanding mind and heart in order that he may know how to bring his pupils "into the vicinity where God himself may speak through the Bible."

3. To Make Thorough Preparation

In his book Lift Up Your Eyes, Lewis J. Sherrill reports on a four-year survey made by a Presbyterian (Southern) body regarding Sunday school work. This is a description of the "average teacher" based on the survey findings:

The teacher in four instances out of five is a woman. She is about forty-five years of age, the mother of two children, has had one year of college, but no teaching experience except that gained in her own church school. She was asked to teach in her teens but has never had any formal course in leadership education. In preparation for class, she spends less than one hour each week, usually on Saturday night. She relies entirely upon her Bible and quarterly and has read no book or article on Christian faith in the past year. She regularly arrives late at church school and is absent about ten Sundays a year. She makes little use of modern methods in her class but nevertheless feels that her work is a success more often than she feels that it is a failure. She attributes her success to her thorough and regular preparation.[7]

How does this portrait compare with that of the average teacher in a Southern Baptist Sunday school? Does he spend *more* than an hour in lesson preparation each week? How much studying has he done within the last year to enrich his Christian faith and to improve his skill as a teacher?

A teacher is not ready to handle any lesson with maximum effectiveness unless he approaches it with a vastly richer context at his command than he will be able to use, and yet with a pretty definite idea of what context he actually intends to use.[8]

In an effort to raise the level of teaching in the average church by the average teacher, the weekly officers and teachers' meeting is being stressed. The Standard of Excellence magnifies participation in this meeting and in special teacher-training opportunities at least once each year. The subject is important enough for a whole chapter in this book to be devoted to a discussion of effective lesson preparation (chap. 5).

Though teaching in secular schools is not all that it might be, certainly teacher preparation standards are kept relatively high in an effort to improve the quality of instruction pupils receive. What must the Intermediate, accustomed to well-prepared teachers in public school, think about poorly prepared Sunday school lessons? Does he spend the same time and effort in studying his Sunday school lesson that he spends in preparing a lesson for day school? Not unless he has a Sunday school teacher who makes comparable preparation. Academic degrees are not required or necessarily needed for one to teach effectively in a Sunday school, but good, honest preparation *is* essential.

4. *To Understand Teaching-Learning Principles*

In addition to knowing his pupils and his subject matter, an effective teacher understands, to some degree at least, how people learn best. He realizes that something has to happen within the person's being (his mind and heart), and he understands ways of helping that "something" to happen.

Certain conditions block learning, while others encourage it. These comments are meant as a mere prelude to a later discussion of teaching-learning principles in chapter 4.

5. *To Use Good Teaching Techniques*

Sometimes teachers who know a lot about the theory of learning do a very poor job of teaching because they do not vary their teaching technique. They are wedded to one way of teaching (so-called). That one way often is lecturing.

It is true that the teacher is not responsible for making pupils learn. He is, however, responsible for the kind of preparation he makes and for the teaching techniques he uses. And it is also true that the better the teaching, the better the opportunity the Holy Spirit has to bring about conversion and growth.

Help in this area will be given later, but in a list of Sunday school teacher needs, the use of good techniques could not be omitted.

6. *To Lead an Exemplary Life*

A bright senior said, "Our greatest problem is being told what to do by adults without ever being shown 'how' in most instances. We can follow a good example better than a good lecture."[9]

Add to the above statement this one made by Dwight L. Moody: "No man can lead another closer to God than he himself is living." The Sunday school teacher who wants to have a good influence over his pupils must, first of all, *be* a good person. He cannot be perfect, for he, too, is a sinner redeemed by God's grace. But his personal life must be clean. His business relations must be honest. He must be faithful to his church and genuinely concerned about the welfare of his fellow men. A teacher of Intermediates must heed Paul's admonition to Titus: "In all things shewing thyself a pattern of good works" (Titus 2:7).

FOR FURTHER CONSIDERATION

1. Underscore the contrasts in the description of the ideal teacher quoted on page 11.
2. List three of your worst traits as a person and three of your worst as a teacher. Why did you have to think before answering?
3. What factors should a person consider before agreeing to teach Intermediates?

---

[1] Lin Yutang, *The Wisdom of Confucius* (New York: Random House, Inc., 1938), p. 247. Used by permission.

[2] Billie Davis, "I Was a Hobo Kid," *Saturday Evening Post,* Dec. 13, 1952. Used by permission of the author.

[3] Ruth Strang, *The Adolescent Views Himself* (New York: McGraw-Hill Book Co., Inc., 1959), p. 512. Used by permission.

[4] Gesell, Ilg, Ames, *Youth* (New York: Harper and Brothers, 1956), p. 452. Used by permission.

[5] Gilbert Highet, *The Art of Teaching* (New York: Vintage Books, 1956), p. 13. Used by permission of Alfred A. Knopf.

[6] Arthur Jersild, *The Psychology of Adolescence,* (New York: The Macmillan Co., 1957), p. 13.

[7] James D. Smart, *The Teaching Ministry of the Church* (Philadelphia: The Westminster Press, 1954), p. 74. Used by permission.

[8] James L. Mursell, *Successful Teaching* (New York: McGraw-Hill Book Co., Inc., 1954), p. 329. Used by permission.

[9] Ruth Strang, *op. cit.,* p. 377. Used by permission.

LET'S TALK ABOUT YOU

As a Sunday School Worker

Answer each question by putting a dot in the correct column opposite it. If you practically always do the thing mentioned or possess the quality indicated, put the dot under "Habitually." If not, put the dot in the column that best represents you.

	1 Habitually	2 Sometimes	3 Never
1. Are you regular in Sunday school attendance?			
2. Do you arrive 15 minutes before starting time?			
3. Do you notify the proper one in advance when you have to be absent?			
4. Do you contact your absentees?			
5. Do you visit in the home of each pupil?			
6. Do you have class meetings and socials?			
7. Do you co-operate in department-wide activities?			
8. Do you keep your classroom looking neat?			
9. Do you make thorough preparation for your work on Sunday morning?			
10. Do you consider the needs and interests of each pupil when you make your plans?			
11. Do you plan for interesting use of the Bible in class?			
12. Do you recognize and commend good work?			
13. Do you plan varied opportunities for pupils to participate?			
14. Are you helping pupils find guidance in God's Word?			
15. Are you the type person pupils will bring their problems to?			
16. Are you influencing pupils to attend preaching services?			
17. Do you read your Bible and pray daily?			
18. Are you training yourself to be a better worker?			
19. Are you concerned about leading lost people to Christ?			
20. Are you convincing pupils that Christ means a lot to you personally?			

Give yourself 5 for each point in column 1; 2 for each in column 2. Subtract 5 for each point in column 3 ("Never").

CHAPTER 3

I. ARE INTERESTED IN THEMSELVES
1. Physical Changes Taking Place
2. The "Self"
3. Personality Development

II. ARE CONCERNED ABOUT RELATIONSHIPS
1. With Their Peers
2. With Their Parents
3. With God

III. ARE DREAMING ABOUT THE FUTURE
1. Schooling
2. Vocation
3. Marriage and Family

IV. ARE FACING CERTAIN DEVELOPMENTAL TASKS
1. To Accept a Changed Physique
2. To Become Emancipated from Parents
3. To Achieve Scholastic Success
4. To Get Along with Age Mates of Both Sexes
5. To Develop a Sense of Social Responsibility
6. To Develop a Christian Philosophy of Life
7. To Consider Their Lifework

3

The Teens We Teach

THE Intermediates themselves have been in the forefront of all that has been said thus far. The concept of teaching included them: *A co-operative enterprise of pupil, teacher, and the Holy Spirit resulting in conversion and growth.* The long-range objectives considered in chapter 1 are learning goals which we (their teachers) hope pupils will set for themselves and will let us help them to reach. Our consideration of the teacher was from the angle of the kind of person one must be if he is to do a good job of teaching Intermediates in Sunday school. So we have already been thinking a great deal about the teens we teach, but this chapter will focus on them somewhat in detail.

It is impossible ever to understand another human being perfectly, but there are some well-established facts about adolescents in general which will enable us to have a better understanding of our individual pupils.

I. ARE INTERESTED IN THEMSELVES

"I would like you to help me with a problem. For the last month or two I've felt different. I don't know how to explain it but I just don't feel the same. I just feel different, and I don't know why. I am 13 years old. Please answer as soon as possible."

So wrote an Intermediate girl to the counselor whose column formerly appeared in the Southern Baptist teen-age magazine, *Upward.* This girl did not know what was happening or why, but she was so deeply concerned about herself that she wanted an immediate reply to her letter!

Adolescents are concerned about—

1. *Physical Changes Taking Place*

Someday Gail will realize (probably she suspected when she wrote the letter) that her strange feeling was related to changes taking place within her body as she was beginning to emerge from childhood into adulthood: silent, maybe imperceptible, but powerful changes.

> The most important single feature of adolescent development consists of changes that take place in the young person's body. Before these changes occur the adolescent is a child. When they have taken place the young man and the young woman are able to have children.[1]

The maturing of the sex organs, commonly referred to as puberty, is accompanied by observable physical change: change in height, weight, body build, voice, and facial appearance. Teen-agers not merely are conscious of their changing appearance but are also conscious of the fact that other people notice the changes, too. As a result, many become self-conscious and ill at ease. Some even become frightened and develop guilt feelings because they do not realize that these changes are normal, desirable, and God-intended.

> Suddenly finding that well-oiled machine that was his body as a child turned into an unco-ordinated monster, the boy or girl reacts with fright and nervousness. In turn, these reactions feed back into the physical system, causing more awkwardness and greater physical discomfort.[2]

Maturation (the process of maturing) does not take place at the same rate for all people. Girls, for instance, ordinarily mature two years earlier than boys. Slow maturing boys may be fifteen or sixteen before their voices begin to change, while early maturers boom bass notes at thirteen. If this difference in growth rate is very marked, some teen-agers get the idea that they aren't normal. Even those who aren't harassed by thoughts of abnormality have problems. At least half of the teen-age population wants to gain or to lose weight. Bad complexion is a problem for many, too.

Contrary to ideas that were current a generation ago, however, adolescence is not always a turbulent period.

It has been estimated that approximately nine-tenths of adolescents pass through this period without permanent emotional disturbances. . . . Whether they do or not depends on the nature and intensity of their earlier experiences, their level of aspiration, their resources for coping with the problems and conflicting goals, their ability to appraise themselves, and their frustration tolerance. Their adjustment also depends on whether the home, the school, and the wider environment facilitate or complicate the normal process of coping with new sensations, desires, and experiences.[3]

You and I as Sunday school teachers are a part of the "wider environment" who should help youngsters to understand and to appreciate the changes taking place within their bodies, which are so fearfully and so wonderfully made (Psalm 139:14).

2. The "Self"

"Self" is another term hard to define because it involves so much. Let's think of it as the inner being—that part of the person included when he uses the pronouns "I" or "me."

During adolescence, a youngster begins for the first time to wonder seriously about his "self": who he is, why he was born, what other people think of him, what kind of man or woman he will turn out to be. As he learns more about the universe, he begins to wonder where he, one little insignificant human being, fits into the picture.

The same teen-ager may actually have several different selves. One of these is the image he has of himself now—the kind of fellow he believes himself to be. Another image is what *he* thinks *other people* think about him. A third one is the kind of person he would really like to be: his ideal self.

Each idea or image is influenced by the other two. For instance, if a person believes that his age mates dislike him or make fun of him, or if he believes that his parents are sorry that they ever had him, he may lose his self-esteen. He may even hate himself or have so little regard for himself that he doesn't care what happens. There is a definite relationship between delinquency and a person's idea about the self.

Many times when adolescents appear to be moody and brooding, they are struggling to understand the self, which has suddenly become a new concept to them. Their hero-worship tendency is a part of their struggle in self understanding, for they pick out the kind of person they would like to be or even imagine themselves to be. Likewise, adolescent daydreams are related to this new awareness of self.

Danger lies ahead for the Intermediate who becomes too preoccupied with self thoughts. He needs worthy heroes to emulate and wholesome, creative ways of finding success and satisfaction. Do you begin to sense the way in which the objectives of Christian education sketched in chapter 1 (part 5, for instance) are directly related to Intermediate needs and interests?

3. *Personality Development*

Though personal qualities and personality are not precisely the same, the two are closely related. Personality may be thought of as a composite of everything making up a person's way of life, including his mannerisms, disposition, and character qualities.

Whatever personality is, it is important to teen-agers because of their association of personality with popularity. If left up to many adolescents, the high school curriculum would put more emphasis on personality development than on academic subjects or vocational skills. There is, of course, a relationship between personality and social acceptance, but not always are desirable inner qualities the factors that make a person popular.

Since an estimated 10 per cent of all teen-agers have rather serious personality difficulties, it behooves Sunday school teachers to be concerned about the mental health of pupils and to try to help them develop the ability and courage and self-confidence to recognize their problems and to solve them satisfactorily.

II. Are Concerned About Relationships

The child is not primarily concerned about ideas, ideals, principles, or values, but he is concerned chiefly about his relationships to others: his parents, his friends, his neighbors, and God. What he wants to know more than anything else is that he is loved and accepted.[4]

Of great importance to adolescents is their relationship—

1. With Their Peers

What other teen-agers (his peers or age mates) think of him is much more important to an Intermediate than what any adult thinks.

There are few things an adolescent prizes more than to be accepted by his peers, and few misfortunes are more poignant than to be rejected by those whose friendship he desires. The companionship of friendly persons is very pleasant in itself and to be accepted by them brings, in addition, a gratifying assurance of one's own worth.[5]

That's why 60 per cent say that they want to make new friends and why 54 per cent want people to like them better. High on the list of questions which teen-agers propose are these: How get a date? What do on a date? How get the kids to like me more?

Their peer relations, especially with the opposite sex, make social activities very attractive to youngsters. They want to be together! Boy-girl relationships also inspire girls to want to be pretty and boys to want to be strong.

Peer relations make it very hard for the Intermediate not to fall in and do what everybody else is doing or wear the type clothes everybody else is wearing.

It was because of peer relation this letter (with its typical teen-age spelling) was written and signed by five boys:

> We, the members of Mr. O'Rork's 14 year old boy's sunday school class, do, being of sound mind and body, make this petition.
>
> We, the undersigned, do hereby petition the leaders of our department to keep us in one class after our promotion into Intermediate No. II Dept.
>
> The reason being that we are all socially, emotionally, and mentally adjusted to each other and feel that future separation will cause an acute case of social malajustment.

A thoughtful superintendent treated the boys' request with sincere respect but explained to them that growth comes through making new adjustments, and that by being placed in separate classes at promotion time, they would grow in their ability to achieve social adjustments.

2. With Their Parents

The relationship of a child to his parents undergoes significant changes during adolescence. No longer is he completely dependent upon them; neither has he achieved complete independence from them. His relation to his parents is one of his chief concerns, though at times his conduct seems to say that he wishes he did not have to fool with his family at all.

This relationship is complicated by the fact that the youngster needs, in fact, he must have if he is to develop normally, latitude to try out his new urge for independence and freedom. At the same time he needs help from his parents and the sense of security which a good home provides.

Even though they frequently make unreasonable demands, argue about the least thing, and criticize at length the way their parents act or dress, teen-agers do really want to please Mother and Dad.

In spite of the fact (according to findings reported in *The American Teenager*) 25 per cent think that their parents do not understand them and 10 per cent think parents are too bossy, more than 50 per cent indicated that in time of trouble they would turn first to their parents for help. Whereas 4 out of 5 say that parents underestimate their maturity, 33 per cent turn right around and indicate that they want more parental guidance.

So, even though they must take second place to peers, parents are important to adolescents.

3. *With God*

Are you surprised to know that the relationship of a youngster to his parents has a definite bearing upon his personal attitude toward God? According to Jersild, the typical adolescent is religious.[6] More than 90 per cent indicate that they believe in God. But just how meaningful that relationship is depends a great deal upon the experiences the Intermediate has had in growing up. For instance, a feeling of hostility toward parents can condition youngsters so that they do not want to have anything to do with God—at least not in an intimate, personal way.

But for the average person, these teen years are a time of searching into the realm of the spiritual and a time of commitment.

As a part of his search, the Intermediate may question some of the religious teachings he has accepted heretofore without question.

This newly strange body of theirs is the battleground for spiritual upheaval. Mother and Dad fall off their pedestals. They *don't* know everything after all—they're not always right. Maybe teachers are wrong, then, too. Maybe—dare they think it?—maybe even the church is wrong! [7]

[Questions may] stem from inability to reconcile certain facts with childhood beliefs. This conflict is intensified by adults who represent science as inimical [opposed] to religion. Actually some of the most able scientists are deeply religious and humble. They feel that science has not invalidated the simple biblical statement, "In the beginning, God. . . ." [8]

The fact that teen-agers care enough and are becoming mature enough to think things through for themselves is no cause for alarm. It is an encouraging sign. As they find answers to their questions, their relationship with God will be more meaningful than ever. Their faith will be stronger.

III. Are Dreaming About the Future

Though they may enjoy life every day, Intermediates seem to feel that they are in a transitional period. They look ahead in a way that the Junior never did. Some of their future concerns are—

1. *Schooling*

To hear students talk, one might think that they detest school, but between 75 and 80 per cent indicated in an opinion poll that they actually like it! Seventy-five per cent of those teen-agers are quick to tell you, however, that they do not want to become high school teachers. From a third to a fourth of all teens in school have anxiety about some phase of school life.[9]

Except in areas having a very restricted curriculum, students are confronted with a choice of subjects; whether to participate in extracurricular activities is another concern.

Sometimes school problems are rooted in interpersonal relationships rather than in curriculum, that is, in the relationship of student to teachers or to other students.

One of the big questions an adolescent has to face is whether to go to college after he finishes high school. In increasing numbers high school students plan to go to college. For some, however, the question is whether to quit school and go to work as soon as the law allows or whether to finish high school. Many of those who want to drop out have not received proper encouragement from parents. Others want to quit because they are lazy or bored or do not study well enough to make passing grades.

2. *Vocation*

This excerpt from the letter of a high school student is representative of another concern of adolescents:

> The only problem I have at the present time is the choice of my future occupation. I can't seem to decide what I would like to do. I like to do a great number of things but none of them appeal to me for my life work. I just can't seem to find something to suit me.[10]

Though all better high schools provide vocational counseling and aptitude tests for students, pupil concern about lifework is not lessened. Nearly half of present-day teen-agers have no idea what career to follow. But all agree about one thing: They should be allowed to make the choice themselves.

3. *Marriage and Family*

The development of the sex organs is accompanied by strong attraction to the opposite sex and by thoughts of getting married and having a family of one's own. As the age for marrying has become lower, teen-age youth have brought their questions about sex and marriage out into the open more than they did formerly. But at least a fourth of them still think that their parents are afraid or are embarrassed to discuss sex with them.

> Because a large number of high school students exchange their class rings for wedding rings immediately after graduation [too many aren't even waiting until graduation!], the high school plays an important role in preparing the adolescent for marriage. Courses in family living, in home economics and in personal problems can be most helpful. People who establish and teach such courses should bear in mind, however, that the old "birds and bees" approach became obsolete decades ago. Youngsters can no more build happy homes on a delicate diet of Victorian evasion than they can build healthy bodies by eating nothing but tea and crumpets.[11]

IV. ARE FACING CERTAIN DEVELOPMENTAL TASKS

Enough has been said already about the teens we teach to verify the fact that life is not simple or easy for them, any more than it is for adults. They are already under a great deal of pressure of various sorts. What life does to them in the future (as well as now) will depend a great deal upon what takes place during their teen years as they move from the dependency of childhood to their new relationships and responsibilities of adulthood.

Just as at certain stages of life a child is supposed to be able to do certain physical things, such as sit alone, crawl, and walk, so certain emotional and psychological and spiritual developments are supposed to take place at given stages. Many of the most important developments must be made during adolescence if the person is ever to become mature.

Psychologists call these competencies that are to be acquired at various ages and stages *developmental tasks*.

> A developmental task is a task which arises at or about a certain period in the life of an individual, successful achievement of which leads to his happiness and to success with later tasks, while failure leads to unhappiness in the individual, disapproval by the society, and difficulty with later tasks.[12]

Since we are working with Intermediates, we are concerned primarily about the developments that ought to take place during adolescence. It is our sacred responsibility to try to discover how we as Sunday school teachers can help pupils do the kind of growing that they must do if they aren't to be retarded later. All that has been said thus far about teen-agers has been leading up to this very point: our part in helping until "we all come in the unity of the faith, and of the knowledge of the Son of God, unto a perfect man, unto the measure of the stature of the fulness of Christ: that we henceforth be no more children, tossed to and fro, and carried about with every wind of doctrine . . . ; but speaking the truth in love, may grow up into him in all things, which is the head, even Christ" (Eph. 4:13–15).

During our Bible study period each Lord's Day and during our weekday activities, there will come teachable moments when we can help the Intermediate—

1. To Accept a Changed Physique

Man, because he was created in the image of God, is of infinite worth, and the body, in which the inner being lives, is likewise sacred. The teen-ager needs to recognize that the changes taking place in his physique are leading up to man's most sacred physical potential, procreation, and to develop a reverent attitude toward God's pattern for parenthood.

Such a concept will remove fear and will help him to direct the sex urge toward worthwhile activities rather than toward sexual experimentation that will leave marks of guilt and shame.

In a sense a teen-ager is a new person with a new role to play. As he increases in physical strength, more is expected of him in other areas. He needs to accept the fact that changes in physique should be accompanied by an increased sense of responsibility, self-control, and ability to think things through and make decisions for himself.

2. *To Become Emancipated from Parents*

As has been said earlier, adolescents are concerned about their relationship to their parents. What development should take place in that relationship during teen years if adult maturity is to be achieved?

Broken homes are often traceable to the fact that the husband or wife is still so emotionally dependent upon one or both parents that he or she is not capable of making a good marriage. The man who is still tied to his mother's apron strings doesn't make a successful husband or a good father. After marriage is usually too late for the string to be cut. The severing should have taken place during adolescence.

In an effort to gain independence, an Intermediate sometimes cuts himself off from his parents or becomes antagonistic toward them for treating him like a child. It is easy for conflict to arise between them over such things as the use of the car, the hour for getting in at night, or the friends teens choose. Sometimes a youngster deliberately ignores or defies his family in an effort to gain status with his peers. A certain amount of conflict is inevitable because, on the one hand, the Intermediate wants and needs his parents; on the other hand, he cannot become independent without practicing his freedom.

The role of the Sunday school teacher will be to help parents and youngsters try to see both sides, never losing sight of the fact that emotional independence does not mean less love of parent for child or *vice versa*. It simply means a more mature kind of love on the part of each. It doesn't mean that the Intermediate is discarding the ideals and standards of his parents. It means that he is thinking things through for himself and is developing his own sense of values. He ought to be permitted to do so without being made to feel that he is betraying his parents or being disloyal to his family.

3. *To Achieve Scholastic Success*

Our culture being what it is today, formal schooling is necessary for the happiness and success of an individual. The teen years in school are vital ones, whether they are the last the youngster will spend in school or whether they are preparatory to college.

A Sunday school teacher can conscientiously try to help his pupils achieve this developmental task. The mind, like the body, is God-given and should be developed for the glory of God and the good of others, as well as for the satisfaction of the individual himself.

(1) If scholastic success is achieved, the pupil will have to assume responsibility. Too often students blame the teacher or the textbook cr the lack of time for study. If this immature tendency is not controlled, they will go through life blaming someone else for their lack of success.

(2) A student who is to achieve scholastic success cannot be satisfied to get by with the minimum. Self-respect demands that a person do his best. Cheating, though it may result in good grades, does not meet this demand either. Scholastic success means more than a grade, though all factors being equal, the grade is an indication of the quality of work.

(3) Learning, not a mark, should be the goal.

4. *To Get Along with Age Mates of Both Sexes*

The Sunday school teacher should have a part in helping pupils achieve social success, as well as scholastic success. Unless some important learnings in human relations take place during teen years, these pupils will grow up to be social misfits.

Teen-agers have a lot to teach each other. Peer discipline is often more effective than parental, school, or church discipline. An adolescent is such a conformist that he doesn't want to go against the crowd. For that reason he limits his behavior to what is acceptable to his peers. The results can be quite good. There are times, however, when a Christian boy or girl needs to go counter to what the crowd thinks and does. When a teachable moment arrives, the Sunday school teacher may help him to identify such times and to build up the courage that will be needed to stand alone.

Many adults are trying "to buy their way" today because they did not learn as teen-agers a better basis for getting along with people. They did not learn that what one *is* is so much more important than what one *has*.

Because of the awakened interest in the opposite sex, adolescence is the time for young folk to learn the "feelings" of life as well as the facts of life. When asked to write a short composition on the subject of what made him tick, one youngster wrote: "What makes me tick? I have an idea it is girls." A sixteen-year-old wrote: "My biggest problem is Women I can't figure them out." [13] Wholesome social and recreational activities are necessary if boys and girls are to grow in understanding and proper appreciation of each other. But the "tick" or "kick" Intermediates get out of being with the opposite sex should never be divorced from the Christian ideals for marriage and family life in the future.

5. *To Develop a Sense of Social Responsibility*

You have known people who act as if the world owes them a living. They are concerned about getting, never about giving. As teen-agers they failed to develop a sense of social responsibility, and they haven't yet learned that they are their brother's keepers.

During adolescence, emotions are intensified, and the young person has an increased capacity for understanding the feelings of another. He can identify himself with the sufferer in a motion picture or book. Even a thirteen-year-old is disturbed about slums and poverty and sick people. He needs also to learn to share feelings of love and joy. Jersild defines "compassion" as the fellowship of feeling and then says:

> Compassion is the ultimate and most meaningful expression of emotional maturity. . . . It is . . . through compassion that a person achieves the highest peak and the deepest reach in his search for self-fulfilment.[14]

The Intermediate who develops a feeling of compassion, best exemplified in Jesus himself, will develop a strong sense of social responsibility. The girl who wrote the following paragraph had achieved this particular developmental goal:

> I would like to be fair and just in my judgment of others. I want always to remember that we are all imperfect and can make mistakes. I want to be kind and helpful to all persons. I'd like to have other people think I am like this. I would like to become a person who could bring joy and happiness to others. I don't particularly want to become a famous person. My goal in life is to become a missionary.[15]

6. *To Develop a Christian Philosophy of Life*

One's philosophy is molded by what one believes. It is greatly influenced by what he believes to be important. If a big car, an expensive house in an exclusive suburb, smart clothes, and elaborate entertaining are all-important to a person, he has a materialistic philosophy of life. "Things" are of greatest value to him.

Teen years are the best time for one to learn a Christian sense of values. The training which the youngster has had up until that time and that which he gets during Intermediate years will enable him to react personally to ideas and ideals which have become a part of his heritage and to come up with a philosophy of his own. His ideas will expand and deepen as time goes by, but it is important that the basis be strengthened during the formative adolescent years.

Christian faith is the source of Christian philosophy. The

teachings of the Book, rather than socially accepted practices, are the standard by which one should measure his attitude and actions. Sometimes the practices approved of and engaged in by a person's own parents may not coincide with the moral and ethical standards of Christ. In such instances, young people have a difficult choice to make. For example, social drinking may be endorsed by a teen-ager's parents and condemned by the teachings of his church. Whether he follows the example of his parents or the precepts of his Sunday school teacher will depend upon his being able to relate the Christian standard to himself. In order to accept the Christian ideal as his behavior guide, he will have to develop personal convictions about the danger and evils of beverage alcohol.

If our faith as their church leaders is deep and sure and if our actions are consistent with what we profess to believe, we can help our pupils to arrive at these biblical conclusions: A human being is a creature of God, made to belong to God's family; but by choice he broke that relationship. It must be through his personal choice that the relationship is restored. Man's happiness depends upon that restoration.

7. To Consider Their Lifework

As was pointed out earlier in the chapter, few teen-agers know positively what their lifework will be, but all are interested in some aspect of a vocational choice. Though few during Intermediate years may make final decisions, it is time for them to be giving serious consideration to lifework. Six months after finishing high school, at least a third of the graduates will be holding down jobs of some sort. In many instances they will have accepted whatever came along without having given enough thought and planning and prayer to making a wise choice.

In order to choose wisely, every individual should consider whether he has skill or the potential skill to fulfil the requirements of the vocation he is interested in. He ought to know the opportunities the job offers in order to decide whether he would be satisfied with that particular work.

Certainly a Christian ought to seek the leadership of the Lord and feel the definite leading of God as he pursues his vocational interests.

FOR FURTHER CONSIDERATION

1. Share with the group the title and theme of some good article or book on adolescence which you have read recently.
2. Recall conversations you have heard recently as teens talked informally among themselves. What did they discuss?
3. How does your experience with Intermediates reflect on the general feeling among adults that adolescents are irresponsible?
4. Describe a church recreational program that would contribute to the physical, social, and spiritual development of Intermediates.

---

[1] Arthur T. Jersild, *The Psychology of Adolescence* (New York: The Macmillan Co., 1957), p. 28. Used by permission.

[2] H. H. Remmers and D. H. Radler, *The American Teenager* (Indianapolis: The Bobbs-Merrill Co., Inc., 1957), p. 41. Used by special permission of publishers.

[3] Ruth Strang, *The Adolescent Views Himself* (New York: McGraw-Hill Book Co., Inc., 1957), p. 133. Used by permission.

[4] Bernhard W. Anderson in curriculum study sessions, Buck Hill Falls, Pennsylvania, 1958.

[5] Arthur T. Jersild, *op. cit.*, p. 209.

[6] *Ibid.*, p. 330.

[7] Remmers and Radler, *op. cit.*, p. 33. Used by permission.

[8] Strang, *op. cit.*, p. 121. Used by permission.

[9] Remmers and Radler, *op. cit.*, chap. 5. Used by permission.

[10] *Ibid.*, p. 120. Used by permission.

[11] *Ibid.*, p. 149. Used by permission.

[12] Robert J. Havighurst, *Developmental Tasks and Education* (New York: Longmans Green and Co., Inc., 1950), p. 2. Used by permission.

[13] Remmers and Radler, *op. cit.*, p. 76. Used by permission.

[14] Jersild, *op. cit.*, p. 201. Used by permission.

[15] Strang, *op. cit.*, p. 72. Used by permission.

CHAPTER 4

I. LEARNING, A CREATIVE PROCESS

II. NECESSARY FACTORS IN LEARNING
1. Ability to Learn (Maturation)
2. Desire to Learn (Motivation)

III. LEARNING SKILLS OF INTERMEDIATES
1. An Understanding of Relationships
2. Ability to Handle Abstract Ideas
3. Ability to Communicate Ideas
4. Ability to Solve Problems
5. Ability to Make Decisions

IV. DIRECTIVES BASED ON LEARNING PRINCIPLES
1. Help Pupils Work Out Significant Learning Goals
2. Create a Situation Conducive to Learning
3. Start Where the Pupil Is
4. Guide Through Pupil Experiences

4

Partners in Learning

TEACHING is a co-operative enterprise, and so is learning. In a sense, learning is the other side of the coin, for real teaching has not been done until learning takes place.

The question before us, then, is this: What is the teacher's part in the learning experience of pupils? In other words, how can a Sunday school teacher best co-operate with God to help pupils learn?

The pupil himself is responsible for learning. No one can do it for him. But the teacher is responsible for directing him so that he can and will learn. His job may be described briefly as assisting pupils to learn.

In order to direct ably, the teacher must have a store of knowledge to draw upon. Among other things he must realize something of the nature of learning.

I. LEARNING, A CREATIVE PROCESS

Learning is a dynamic process, not a static one. Something happens in the mind and heart of the learner. He takes facts and ideas which the teacher shares with him and re-works them or translates them into his own experience. Learning does not take place at the transmission level but at the *translation* level as the pupil becomes aware of needs (some he probably hasn't even been conscious of before) and tries to discover the solution to his problem.

Helping pupils sense spiritual needs which they are only dimly aware of is one of the creative opportunities of a Sunday school teacher. At the transmission level a teen-ager may be told about the joy another has experienced through some act of Christian service. But that Intermediate will not really *know* that joy until he has shared a part of himself and of his own possessions with another.

II. NECESSARY FACTORS IN LEARNING

When viewing the process from the learner's standpoint, a teacher realizes that two factors are necessary before a person can learn.

1. *Ability to Learn* (*Maturation*)

In the first place, the pupil must be able to learn; he must have learning capacity. Psychologists call this ability "maturation" (coming from the same root as the word "mature"). A teacher used a simpler term to describe learning ability: "can do."

Man, because he was created in the image of God, has the ability to learn. (Only a relatively small percentage of people are so retarded mentally that they are not able to participate in a learning process. Special plans have to be made for those exceptional ones.) The central nervous system of a human being is so constructed that he has the power to think, reason, remember, and imagine. These abilities are necessary, God-given learning tools.

2. *Desire to Learn* (*Motivation*)

An Intermediate's learning tools, however, will remain unused unless he *wants* to learn. The "can do" is useless without the "want to," or without motivation. A person must feel within himself the urge to participate, else all the teacher's effort is useless. In a recent survey this question was asked of Intermediate workers: What can be done in pupil and teacher materials and by teachers in class to motivate pupils to study Sunday school lessons seriously? Too many of the workers replied, "I wish I knew!" implying that nothing can be done. Maybe the situation is hopeless in a few instances. But instead of giving in to passive pupil resistance, the Sunday school teacher needs to discover ways of encouraging pupils to want to learn.

He can do so sometimes by anticipating a *future need* the youngster will experience, even though at present he is not at all conscious of that need. *Curiosity* and *suspense* are often effective in motivating learning. A satisfying or *successful experience* inspires a person to want to know more. A noted educator has said, "A sure way to relax human character is to arouse fine intentions without permitting them to be carried out in action." We may add to his thought by saying that a sure way to stifle learning interest is to set worthy goals and arouse deep emotion without guiding pupils to participate in a culminating, satisfactory activity.

Success on a spiritual level brings the greatest satisfaction of all. So an opportunity to apply a biblical truth in a personal way is a strong motivating force in the life of an Intermediate.

Motivation as applied particularly to the realm of Sunday school teaching will be discussed and illustrated later in connection with teaching plans. The purpose of this brief discussion now is to identify it as an important aspect of the learning process and to establish a principle of learning based on it, namely, that motivation, which creates interest, is essential in the learning process.

III. Learning Skills of Intermediates

A pupil's learning ability should be equal to the learning task confronting him. He should not be asked to learn something that is beyond his capacity. Neither should he be bored by being asked to do something too elementary. So we who work with Intermediates need to know just what we can expect of them as far as learning abilities are concerned.

Since no two teen-agers are exactly alike, it is not wise

to set up a list of learning skills and expect all pupils to be able to perform them with the same degree of efficiency. Not all pupils have developed at the same rate of speed; some also have less innate intelligence.

However, it is important for the teacher to know the kind of learning experiences Intermediates in general are capable of having and are interested in participating in. Certain things can be expected of them now that could not have been when they were Juniors.

1. An Understanding of Relationships

We have noted already an increasing desire on the part of an adolescent to understand himself and other people. He, then, is more capable of understanding relationships than he has been before: the relationships of people, of things, of events, of moral rules to conduct, and of cause and effect.

As their sphere of interest expands, their power of understanding and appreciation increases. They are capable of feeling a concern as Christians for the spiritual and physical welfare of others—far away, as well as near at hand.

The testimonies of missionaries of our denomination, as well as of others, indicate that the majority of missions volunteers first felt their call to Christian service during their teen years.

Because of their maturing thoughts and feelings, Intermediates are capable of experiencing a vital personal relationship with Christ as their Lord as well as Saviour. They can likewise grow in their appreciation of Christian fellowship and of the importance of associating with people who will help them grow in Christlikeness.

2. Ability to Handle Abstract Ideas

A young child thinks best in concrete terms. He can see that an apple in one hand added to an apple in the other hand equals two apples. But the junior or senior high math student can handle the symbols x and y in his algebra problems. He can think in abstract and symbolic terms.

These same youngsters can understand that baptism is more than an act transpiring in the baptistry. It symbolizes the burial of the sinful self and the resurrection of the new person in Christ. Jesus the Good Shepherd suggests to the Intermediates the loving concern of our Lord, not just some artist's conception of Jesus with a lamb in his arms. They can define such qualities as courage and loyalty, for their mental maturity enables them to handle abstractions.

3. Ability to Communicate Ideas

Intermediates, as a rule, are able to make themselves understood. They can communicate. Because they like to share ideas, they enjoy discussion, debates, and panels. Many of them take pride in speaking in public and in giving reports before a group. Others really enjoy trying to express themselves through dramatic roles.

Secular school teachers verify the fact that some, particularly thirteen-year-old girls, like to express themselves in writing, especially if the writing is autobiographical in nature. Counselors who write columns for daily papers receive many, many letters from teen-agers.

Sunday school teachers who do not plan so that pupils will have an opportunity to communicate their ideas are overlooking a learning skill which could be used to the advantage of the entire group.

4. Ability to Solve Problems

In a sense, all learning is problem-solving, for it "is the means by which man adjusts to his environment through the modification of his behavior." [1] Without problems, or something to upset the *status quo*, one goes his merry way without learning anything new. When confronted by an obstacle, however, a person has to do something.

Intermediates have the maturity to face a situation, recognize the problem, and to figure out how to solve it. For instance, this may be a *situation:* A family moves into a new community, and the teen-ager in that family is cut off from his former friends. The *problem* is: how to get in with "the crowd" in the new community. The *solution* may be: to go out for football at school, to become active in a Sunday school class and an Intermediate union at church, and to get a job delivering papers in the neighborhood.

Now an adolescent himself is capable of recognizing these steps as a means of getting to know people and of solving his problem of needing friends. The parents of a younger child might have to take the initiative, but the Intermediate can act for himself.

5. *Ability to Make Decisions*

Closely related to the learning skill just mentioned is this one: the ability to decide. Emotions (feelings), as well as intellect, are involved in making decisions. And it takes a certain amount of growing up before one is capable of exploring ideas, weighing them, and then deciding what to do in relation to them. A decision reached in such a manner, however, means more than a handed-down or superimposed one.

The Sunday school teacher can depend upon this particular learning skill as he confronts pupils with the question as to what they will do in response to a challenge in God's Word.

IV. DIRECTIVES BASED ON LEARNING PRINCIPLES

Before more is said about an understanding and use of learning principles, let it be understood that though this kind of knowledge is important, it is not the only essential knowledge. A teacher has to know something before he can teach. He has to have some factual knowledge and understanding to share with his class. But a teacher should look upon his knowledge as a means of helping pupils learn, not as an end in itself. Knowledge of biblical content, as well as of teaching technique, should be regarded as tools to help pupils learn.

With that understanding in mind, let's go back to the learning process and consider some directives to be followed if teaching is to be effective.

1. *Help Pupils Work Out Significant Learning Goals*

One way of being sure that the class period will be meaningful is to let the group share in formulating learning goals.

This does not mean, however, that lesson quarterlies will be thrown away and that pupils will just decide what they want to talk about. Well-balanced Bible study would never result from any such procedure. But this directive does mean that pupils should have a part in deciding what they would like to get out of a unit of lessons and what approach they would like to take in developing it.

Certainly the teacher, with the help given in his lesson materials, will have to assume the initiative in setting up objectives. But as he opens up the possibilities of the unit to the class, he can motivate them to accept and adapt his thinking so that in the end it will become their own. The teacher can then plan how to help them find answers to the questions *they want answered*. In order to be effective, teaching must be related to felt needs of pupils.

> Unless a person wants to learn, unless something makes a difference to him, unless he has a purpose . . . the things that happen will remain outside of him. He must become involved, or participate, at the level of purpose.[2]

In quite different words, a thirteen-year-old expressed the same idea as that quoted above:

> When I am interested in something I read faster and understand what I read with a feeling I am getting something out of

it. I feel like keeping on with the same subject. And when they ask me a question I have the right answer.

When I am not interested I can't hardly read or understand what I'm studying about. I feel like the period is never going to finish. I feel like I ain't getting nothing out of what I am studying. And I feel lazying, sleepy without energy; can't wait till the period is finished so I can go to the other.[3]

Confidentially, did you ever feel that way about a Sunday school class? Has an Intermediate ever felt like that about *your* class?

2. Create a Situation Conducive to Learning

Sunday school teachers, as well as secular teachers, can help pupils get in the right frame of mind for learning. They can influence learning readiness; they can help bring about teachable moments. And in the case of Intermediates, with a longer concentration span, these teachable moments can be expanded in duration. When interested, even a thirteen-year-old can work at a learning task for twenty-five or thirty minutes at a time.

Let's note some factors that can influence the ease and pleasure with which one learns:

(1) *Physical surroundings.*—The temperature, the light, the orderliness or lack of orderliness, the arrangement of chairs, and the physical relationship of pupils and teacher can influence learning favorably or unfavorably. It is not wise to assume that the custodian will have every Sunday school classroom in perfect order. Teachers themselves need to check on the details before Sunday school begins.

The teacher who sits as one of the group of learners will come much nearer creating the needed "togetherness" than the person who stands and looks down on his class members. The group can learn from other pupils much better if they are sitting facing one another rather than in stiff rows facing the teacher, barricaded behind a table.

(2) *Size and spirit of the class.*—An informal seating arrangement cannot be depended on alone to create an atmosphere conducive to learning. The attitude of the teacher and the attitude of the pupils toward each other are a more important consideration.

If the pupils want to find answers to their questions and to help others find solutions to their problems, and if they are confident that the teacher wants to and can help them in their search, then learning will take place! In a small class (ranging ideally from six to ten pupils), everybody can participate, and the teacher will be better able in a group that size to keep a proper balance between freedom and formality.

(3) *Involvement of the pupil.*—It is possible, though, for a group of friendly people to meet in an ideally equipped classroom with a brilliant teacher and still not learn a thing. Pupils have to become so involved in the process (motivated) that they want to assume their share of the responsibility. Not until the experience begins to mean something to him personally does the pupil really begin to learn.

Ways of getting a class to feel personally involved will be considered in a later chapter.

3. Start Where the Pupil Is

If ability and desire are necessary factors in learning, then the teacher, when making his plans, will have to take into consideration the pupil's maturity so that he can begin where the youngster is. For instance, a teen-ager from a non-Christian home, enrolling in Sunday school for the first time in his life, is not ready to grasp some higher concepts of Christian dedication that another can grasp after being reared in a Christian home and having participated all of his life in church activities.

In order to be able to start where his pupils are, the teacher must know them individually. It is possible to underestimate their readiness and maturity, as well as to overestimate it, and to begin on a level so elementary that pupils never become interested.

The application of this learning principle will also lead the teacher to plan carefully for the beginning step in each lesson procedure. Intermediates sitting in a Sunday school classroom on Sunday morning in their best clothes are not necessarily in a spiritual or learning mood. But the teacher has no choice; he has to take them as they are and try to get them deeply enough interested in the lesson subject that they will want to learn.

4. Guide Through Pupil Experiences

The slogan (so popular a few years ago) "we learn by doing" is true. But *what* one learns depend on what one does! Not all "doing" is profitable. Mere activity or "busy work" has no place in a Sunday school class. But meaningful experience is essential, for it is the only medium through which one really learns.

A person can have a genuine experience as he hears, thinks, and feels. An Intermediate who searches a portion of God's Word to find an answer and then, having found it, weighs it, and decides what he will do in the light of his finding has really undergone an experience. In the process he likely engaged in several activities: Bible reading, asking and answering questions, weighing answers, and then making up his own mind.

It is the teacher's responsibility, then, to plan and organize his lesson materials in such a way that pupils will have experiences to guide them into a better understanding of God and of his purposes for their lives.

The discussion throughout this chapter has pointed up the significance of the words "have experiences." When pupils become aware of problems related to their own lives; when they come to feel that the Bible has something to say which really bears on these problems; and when they are guided in discovering from the Bible truths which really matter, right where Intermediates are living day by day, then pupils will "become involved." They will have experiences which will result in changed attitudes and conduct and will help them to move toward Christian maturity.

FOR FURTHER CONSIDERATION

1. Can *what* one learns be separated from *how* he learns?
2. Comment on the difference between the *transmission* level and the *translation* level in the learning process.
3. Which is a better sign that pupils are learning: knowing the answer to a question or raising a question to be answered? Why?

---

[1] Vernon E. Anderson, *Principles and Procedures of Curriculum Development* (New York: The Ronald Press Co., 1956), p. 104. Used by permission.

[2] Sara Little, *Learning Together in the Christian Fellowship* (Richmond: John Knox Press, 1956), p. 32. Used by permission.

[3] Ruth Strang, *The Adolescent Views Himself* (New York: McGraw-Hill Book Co., Inc., 1957), p. 251. Used by permission.

CHAPTER 5

I. IMPORTANCE OF TIME AND PLACE FOR STUDY

II. WORKING TOOLS
1. Bible
2. Age-Group Curriculum Publications
3. Other Resource Materials

III. STEPS IN LESSON PLANNING
1. Mastering Biblical Content
2. Summarizing Lesson Truth
3. Considering Pupil Needs and Interests
4. Deciding upon Learning Goals
5. Working Out the Teaching Plan
   (Developed in detail in chap. 7)

5

Lesson Preparation

A MAN outstanding in the field of secular education and well informed about all phases of teaching said:

Daily lesson planning and teaching is the most important single aspect of success as a teacher. It is not separate from all other aspects of teaching, but is the place where teachers must be most concerned about doing an adequate and continuously improving job.[1]

Sunday school teachers must also be deeply concerned about preparation each week in anticipation of meeting their classes on Sunday morning. Regardless of how important out-of-class contacts are (and they are important), the teacher's major teaching opportunity comes during the time set aside for Bible study each Lord's Day.

So this chapter will be devoted to some suggestions to help teachers do "an adequate and continuously improving job" of preparing the weekly lesson.

I. IMPORTANCE OF TIME AND PLACE FOR STUDY

Most of us work better when we follow some sort of regular routine. Doing so doesn't mean that we lack creativity. It simply means that good habits help us to expedite our responsibilities. Setting a regular time and place for study will, in all probability, result in more effective lesson preparation. Each teacher must decide for himself when that time (rather, when *those times*) will be and what place can best serve his purpose. But the schedule should include study time early in the week, as well as later in the week.

There are several good reasons for beginning preparation early. (1) During the week the teacher will come across material (some of it as current as the daily newspaper) that can greatly enrich the learning experience for himself and his class. (2) Thinking about the lesson (do you know the old term "mulling over it"?) for several days will add mellowness or depth that will be lacking if preparation is postponed until Saturday night. (3) Early preparation is a safeguard against inadequate preparation resulting from unexpected happenings. (4) The one who has his preparation well under way before the midweek officers and teachers' meeting will have something to share with the group, and their contributions to him will be more meaningful also.

How much time should be devoted to lesson study each week? The number of hours depends upon a lot of things, including the training and experience of the teacher, his familiarity with the particular content, and his understanding of his pupils. But even the most experienced Bible student will have to spend hours in preparation in order to make a fresh approach and the right approach for his particular pupils. A class can soon tell whether the teacher has made new preparation. Remember, Intermediates respect the teacher "who can serve ample intellectual fare."

The place for study will likewise depend upon the individual and his surrounding circumstances. He will need to work where he can spread out his materials without feeling that he is imposing on someone else or that he will be disturbed by others. A place where one can develop "inner quietness," where he can sense the presence of God to an unusual degree is best, wherever that may be. Even though a person may be able to concentrate easily, he will find sitting in the same room where the TV is blaring forth for the entertainment of other members of the family hardly the ideal spot for preparing to teach God's Word.

II. Working Tools

In order to do a good job, every workman needs tools. The qualities Sunday school teachers need in order to be good workmen were discussed in chapter 2. In addition to mental and spiritual equipment, however, teachers need certain concrete materials with which to work.

1. *Bible*

Of first importance in lesson preparation is the Bible itself. It *is* the textbook. Other materials are supplementary.

It is quite desirable for a teacher to have at his disposal when he studies at least two versions or translations. One of these should be the King James and one should be a modern translation. Inasmuch as the usage of many English words has changed since the King James translation was made in 1611, a newer version, such as *The New English Bible* or the Revised Standard Version, will help make obscure passages more readily understood. There are several other good modern translations available under such identifications as these: Williams, Montgomery, Weymouth, Goodspeed, Moffatt, and Phillips.

A Bible containing a few good maps and a limited concordance is desirable for a teacher. But an edition including a great many notes and editorial comments may be more confusing than helpful. The reader should always remember that marginal notes, chapter headings, and any other such features are not a part of the inspired Word. They have been added by an editor in an effort to clarify the biblical text.

2. *Age-Group Curriculum Publications*

The word "curriculum" is a significant one in the realm of education, whether secular or Christian. There was a time when the term referred almost exclusively to textbooks, or at least to printed resource materials. But the concept has been expanded now to include in the curriculum any phase of school life (or Sunday school life) which helps the pupil reach the goals or objectives agreed upon.

In secular school, such things as the counseling program, related work experiences, the library, and the athletic program are considered a part of the curriculum just the same as classroom studies are. Assembly programs, weekday class meetings, the church library, and weekend retreats are in a broader sense a part of the Sunday school curriculum, too, just so long as these activities help achieve the purposes that have been set up for Sunday school. But in our discussion of lesson preparation, let's limit our discussion to printed curriculum materials.

Every teacher, regardless of how resourceful he may be, needs some kind of instructional helps. Textbooks (in our case, the Bible and the teacher and pupil quarterlies) have an important place as aids to learning.

Sunday school lesson courses should meet two criteria: They should be thoroughly Christian, and they should be developmental, that is, adapted to age-group needs and abilities. In order to try to meet the needs of churches of various sizes, the Baptist Sunday School Board provides two lesson courses for Intermediates: Uniform lessons and Cycle Graded lessons.

(1) *Uniform lessons.*—The Uniform series is based on Sunday school lesson outlines formulated by denominational representatives making up the Committee on the Uniform Series. Southern Baptists are represented on the Committee by four age-group editors, the editor in chief of the Sunday school lesson courses, and the editorial secretary of the Baptist Sunday School Board.

The Committee on the Uniform Series maps out areas of biblical content to be studied over a six-year cycle. Each quarter in the cycle is developed by the Committee to this extent only: the selection of a Bible passage (background and print), of an age-group topic, and of a memory selection. Then each participating denomination develops the outline to suit itself. The Committee never moves into the area of interpretation, for biblical interpretation is a denominational responsibility.

Except for an occasional adaptation, Intermediate classes using the Uniform course study the same theme and biblical passages that Young People and Adults (and often Juniors) study. All Intermediates study the same lesson, for there is only one Intermediate pupil book and only one teacher book each quarter. There is, of course, a different set of lessons for each quarter. During the six-year period, a person studying Uniform lessons gets a good view of the Old Testament and of the New, with emphasis on the life of Christ.

(2) *Cycle Graded lessons.*—The outline for the Cycle Graded course (beginning October, 1963) was mapped out at the Baptist Sunday School Board. Staff members at the Board, Sunday school teachers, youth directors, pastors, ministers of education, parents, and public-school teachers were in the group who worked with the age-group editor in creating the outlines. Cycle Graded lessons have been planned specifically with Intermediates in mind, whereas in the over-all plans for the Uniform lessons, other age groups must also be considered. There are, naturally, advantages in a course planned for Intermediates only.

The Cycle Graded course offers another advantage. It gives consideration to the developmental difference between thirteen-year-olds and sixteen-year-olds. The teacher using the Uniform course, prepared for all four Intermediate ages, must do the adapting to his own age group by himself. The Cycle Graded lessons, prepared for only a two-year range, take less adaptation.

The Cycle Graded course consists of sixteen quarters of work, eight of which are used each year. Thirteen's and fourteen's study the same lesson, and fifteen's and sixteen's study the same lesson. The course is divided into Series A and Series B, to be used in alternate years.

In addition to books for pupils and teachers, there are books for superintendents of departments using Cycle Graded lessons. Each of these books contains six months' work so that the superintendent uses two books a year. For each lesson, the superintendent's book carries two definite plans: one for the teaching improvement period of weekly officers and teachers' meeting and one for the assembly program.

During his four years in the Intermediate department, a youngster studying Cycle Graded lessons has excellent Bible coverage, planned in scope and sequence so as to hold his interest and to meet his needs.

Since the same plates are used over a period of years in printing Cycle Graded books, the production cost is spread over a span of years. Thus, it is financially possible (by charging just a little more) to make these materials more attractive in format than a Uniform quarterly can be.

The basic philosophy underlying both Intermediate courses is the same. Often the same writers prepare materials for both. Cycle Graded and Uniform lessons both magnify the Bible. So which course is better for your church depends upon your situation.

Churches with two or four Intermediate departments may use the Cycle Graded lessons easily. It is possible to use them in a department having a class for boys and a class for girls in each age. However, the latter type of department may encounter difficulty in conducting the weekly officers and teachers' meeting, where two different lessons would have to be dealt with each session: Uniform lessons will probably be more effective in such a department.

(3) *Pupil and teacher books.*—In making lesson preparation, every worker should study the material written for pupils, as well as that written for teachers themselves. Each

is written from a different point of view. Studying pupil material will enable the teacher to know what his class member has already learned for himself by reading his lesson. The class period should be devoted to deeper exploration rather than to rehashing what the pupil has already read.

3. *Other Resource Materials*

Though writers and editors try to make teacher and pupil books as comprehensive as possible, we are the first to say to teachers: "Do not limit your preparation to these two sources."

Sunday school teachers will find certain basic materials helpful regardless of the lesson course followed.

(1) *Harmony of the Gospels.*—In preparing to teach a unit on the life of Christ, a teacher will find a harmony most helpful, for he will want to study parallel accounts of the event or discourse as recorded in the Gospels other than the one being featured. A harmony arranges in parallel columns the scriptural accounts so that the similarities and differences can easily be recognized. Robertson's *A Harmony of the Gospels* (compiled by the late Dr. A. T. Robertson of Southern Baptist Theological Seminary) is a well-known one among our constituency. Other harmonies are listed in your *Baptist Book Store Catalog.*

(2) *Bible dictionary.*—A Bible dictionary has the combined features of a dictionary and an encyclopedia. In addition to pronunciation, an explanation (rather than a bare definition) is given for all people, places, and things mentioned in the Bible. Charts explaining biblical weights, measures, distances, as well as dynasties and such, add to usefulness of a dictionary as resource material.

The Westminster Dictionary of the Bible is a good one in the average price range; others of equal merit are available through your Baptist Book Store.

(3) *Concordance.*—A resourceful teacher often uses bibli-

cal references which are not a part of the lesson text itself. Locating desired passages is quite easy with a concordance handy. In it are listed all principal words in the Bible and the reference or references showing where the words are used. *Cruden's Complete Concordance* is a good one.

(4) *Commentary.*—Another source of enrichment is a commentary. Whereas ministers study from sets of commentaries to ascertain the thinking of various scholars, many Sunday school teachers do not feel that they can buy such sets or that they can devote time to such exhaustive study. A one-volume commentary is the tool they need.

In a commentary a section is devoted to each book of the Bible, to each chapter, and to a group of verses, if not to individual verses.

Dummelow's *The One Volume Bible Commentary* is a popular one, for the scholarship on which it is based is not extreme in point of view.

Broadman Comments is an annual commentary published by the Baptist Sunday School Board as a commentary on Uniform lessons for a calendar year. This one, and the annual commentaries published by other denominations or by independent publishers, develops the lesson from an adult point of view. So teachers of Intermediates using Uniform materials would use *Broadman Comments* to enrich background, not as a substitute for age-group periodicals.

(5) *Maps.*—The study of units that are biographical or historical in nature can be greatly enriched by the use of maps. Seeing the location of a town or country in relation to other cities and nations helps an Intermediate to sense its reality. One cannot appreciate properly the ministry of Jesus and the twelve or of Paul and his missionary helpers without maps revealing the location of their activities. A study of Abraham's call and of the Exodus will be much more exciting if pupils can follow the Hebrews on a map.

The following basic maps are recommended for use with Intermediates. They are selected from a series of Broadman Class Maps:

No. 1 "The Biblical World, 2000–1500"
No. 5 "Palestine in the Time of Christ"
No. 6 "The Missionary Journeys of Paul"

III. STEPS IN LESSON PLANNING

Maybe you remember a conversation in *Alice in Wonderland* between Alice and the Cat, which was something like this:

". . . would you tell me, please, which way I ought to go from here?"

"That depends a great deal on where you want to get," said the Cat.

"I don't much care where—" said Alice.

"Then it doesn't matter much which way you go," said the Cat.

". . . so long as I get *somewhere*," Alice added as an explanation.

"Oh, you're sure to do that," said the Cat, "if you only walk long enough."

As you have prepared your Sunday school lesson, have you ever felt like Alice? You want to get somewhere, but you do not know exactly where, and you do not know how to get there.

The five steps which follow should help you know how to prepare more effectively.

1. *Mastering Biblical Content*

Every Sunday school lesson is based on a given portion of God's Word. Sometimes the passages are long (that is, the background Scripture portions to be studied in connection with the lesson are long). At other times, especially when the unit is a topical one (probably dealing with personal problems), the chosen Bible material may be much briefer. But regardless of its length, the Bible passage is of great importance in the lesson development. So a logical first step is to try to master the biblical content.

In order to do so, a teacher will have to read prayerfully the passage or passages several times, particularly the portion chosen for special emphasis (printed in Uniform materials and listed in the Graded). Then should follow a careful study of the expository material in the teacher book, which helps reveal the meaning of the Word. A Bible dictionary or a commentary may be studied to clarify some point not touched upon in the teacher helps.

Whatever the time or procedure involved, the teacher should work on the biblical content until he becomes conscious of the message God is speaking through it.

> We must live with the Bible until it becomes part of us, just as the actor identifies himself with the role that he plays. It is then, perhaps, that the Holy Spirit, breathing through the ancient words of the sacred page, will lead us to know that the "Word of the Lord" spoken by the prophets and embodied in Jesus Christ is actually the deepest interpretation of our own life situation and our world crisis in the twentieth century.[2]

2. *Summarizing Lesson Truth*

Finite beings may not ever be able to comprehend *all* that is contained in a portion of the Word, but teachers can reach a point where they feel that they are ready to proceed to the next stage of preparation. A good test to prove whether that stage of readiness has been attained in mastering biblical content is to try to put into one brief statement the central truth of the chosen Bible passage.

This truth should be stated in terms of present-day experience. For instance, the heart of the message for us in the book of Job may be summarized in some such statement as this: *Humble submission to God in time of suffering leads to a better understanding of God and to a restoration of life's wholeness.*

3. Considering Pupil Needs and Interests

When the mind and heart of the teacher have become saturated with the biblical content and he is able to summarize the truth for himself, then he should begin thinking of his pupils. (If he has not already done so, he should read the lesson development in the pupil book.) In what aspect of this truth are pupils interested? What need could be met through a personal discovery of that truth for themselves? What learning task could it help them fulfil if they appropriated it to themselves?

Effective lesson preparation breaks down at this point for the teacher who doesn't know his pupils. But the teacher who does understand them—their likes and dislikes, their recognized and unrecognized needs, their aspirations and limitations—is ready to move to the next step in his preparation.

4. Deciding upon Learning Goals

As the teacher thinks of his pupils one by one in relation to the central truth of the lesson, he begins to think of what he hopes will happen to them during their learning experience based on this particular portion of God's Word. As his thinking crystallizes, he is really deciding upon the learning goals which he hopes pupils will accept for themselves.

Unless the teaching procedure is developed around certain goals or purposes or aims, the teaching will be aimless, and the outcomes will be accidental.

Since within one small class there will be variety of ability and of need, the learning goals must provide for different levels of experience and different types of experience. The goal for one may be the achievement of a certain skill. For others it may be the acquisition of knowledge or the development of understanding and appreciation. Goals may be expressed in terms of knowing, feeling, doing.

Whatever the goal, it should be so clearly defined that pupils and teachers know the problem confronting them and the direction in which they are moving in an effort to solve it.

Certainly there is no more vital step in lesson preparation than the selection of purpose or the learning goal. It should always be stated from the point of view of the pupil since it describes in a brief summarizing way the change the lesson is designed to bring about in him. For instance, the learning goal in a lesson on Job may be stated like this: *to discover through Job's experiences the secret of being able to endure suffering without cracking up under the strain.*

5. Working Out the Teaching Plan

The success of all that has been done thus far in lesson preparation depends upon this fifth step: working out plans whereby pupils will have the desired experiences, that is, plans whereby pupils will discover the truth of God's Word and will see how they can put it to work in their own lives.

On the one hand we have a given truth; on the other we have a given class. The remaining step in preparation is deciding how to get the two together so that under the leadership of the Holy Spirit real growth will take place.

That's exactly where a teaching plan comes in, and it is such an important phase of preparation and of the class period itself that a whole chapter will be devoted to consideration of it.

FOR FURTHER CONSIDERATION

1. What have you found to be the minimum amount of time needed each week for adequate teaching preparation?

2. What is the most significant difference between the Uniform and the Graded lesson courses?
3. Suggest ways, in addition to weekly lesson study, whereby Sunday school teachers may grow in knowledge and appreciation of biblical content.
4. To what extent should pupils have a part in setting up learning goals?

---

[1] Sam P. Wiggins, *Successful High School Teaching* (Cambridge: The Riverside Press, 1958), p. 202. Used by permission of Houghton Mifflin Co.

[2] Bernhard W. Anderson, *Rediscovering the Bible* (New York: Association Press, 1951), p. 22. Used by permission.

CHAPTER 6

I. METHODS ARE—
1. Not Techniques to Manipulate Pupils
2. Ways of Working Together

II. FACTORS TO CONSIDER IN CHOOSING METHODS
1. Size and Character of the Class
2. Time Available for Teaching
3. Learning Goals
4. Nature of Material
5. The Teacher

III. METHODS EFFECTIVE WITH TEEN-AGERS
1. Lecture
2. Group Discussion
3. Illustration
4. Scripture Searching
5. Question-Answer
6. Assignment (Research and Report)
7. Buzz Session
8. Field Trip and Interview
9. Audio-Visuals
10. Role-playing

6

Methods Illustrated and Evaluated

As WAS SAID in the preceding chapter, a significant part of teacher preparation is the making of a plan to be used as a guide for class activities on Sunday morning. In order to plan how to help pupils learn effectively, a teacher must know something about teaching methods.

I. METHODS ARE—

Before considering specific methods, we should come to a common understanding about the term itself, for "methods" means various things to various people.

1. *Not Techniques to Manipulate Pupils*

In choosing methods to use during a class period, a teacher should not try to think of gimmicks or gadgets to keep pupils busy or to make them respond in an expected way.

Teaching consists of a great deal more than the manipulation of pupils. A class may go through the motions of learning, responding according to the pattern the teacher had worked out, but not learn a thing. A teacher may feel at the end of a smooth-running class period that he has taught a good lesson, when actually he has not taught at all. The quality of pupil experience is the determining factor in evaluating methods.

2. *Ways of Working Together*

Methods are simply ways whereby pupils and teachers work together to reach certain goals. Do you remember this phrase in Confucius' definition of a teacher's task: "He opens the way"? In selecting methods, the teacher decides which technique he thinks will best open up the way for pupils to learn, for, after all, the pupil has to do the learning. It is an inward process.

There is no *one* best method, for there is no one best way of opening up channels of communication. Any method is more effective when used in combination with others so that it does not stand out at all. It may even be hard to identify. But if it motivates a pupil to want to learn or if it provides an answer he has been searching for, then the method is good, regardless.

II. Factors to Consider in Selecting Methods

Certain circumstances have a lot to do with the effectiveness or ineffectiveness of specific methods. Not all ways of opening up learning opportunities are of equal value all the time, for given factors influence the success with which methods can be used.

1. *Size and Character of the Class*

The size of a class, as well as the nature of the group, is a significant factor to consider. Some classes are so large (not Intermediate ones, let us hope!) that the teacher has no choice; he has to lecture. Eight to ten pupils should be considered the maximum for an Intermediate class.

If pupils are near enough the same age to have interests and needs in common, it is easier to decide on methods than if the class is diverse in character. Having the class limited to one sex is an advantage, for some methods that appeal to girls are not effective with boys.

The physical arrangement of the classroom is of importance, too. For instance, teaching opportunities are increased when rooms can be made suitable for the effective use of projected visuals. Nearly all classrooms are too small for motion picture equipment and projection, but not for slides. Some are not large enough to permit pupils to move around freely. Size often rules out methods (such as drama) requiring much open space. Some classes do not have a room of any type!

2. Time Available for Teaching

Time is another factor to be considered. An activity requiring an hour of uninterrupted work would not be a good method to try to use within a thirty-five-minute class period. A lesson well planned will provide for carry-over activities, but there is a big difference between a carry-over and a lesson left suspended in mid-air. Methods should be chosen with the view to leaving pupils with a sense of completion rather than frustration.

3. Learning Goals

What pupils are to learn will be a determining factor in *how* they will best learn. Before attempting to decide on a class procedure, a teacher must know what he hopes will be accomplished. In other words, he must set up learning goals. Once he knows the destination, deciding on a possible route for getting there will be an easier matter.

4. Nature of Material

When Sunday school curriculum materials were limited to a catechism book consisting of brief questions and answers, the teaching methods were limited to rote memory, drill, and questions and answers. The content practically determined the methods of teaching.

In a day when the curriculum is much broader than it was three or four generations ago, the nature of content is still a determining factor in the selection of methods. Sunday school lessons are no longer catechetical in nature; rather, the content is of the problem-solving type, meant to help pupils face moral and spiritual issues for themselves. That being true, recommended teaching methods do not stress drill or rote memorization.

Methods vary as biblical content varies in historical, biographical, or personal problems units. Whereas pupils may want to make a notebook while studying the life of Christ or of Paul, they would not likely care to do so while studying a unit in the area of interpersonal relations.

5. *The Teacher*

The ability, experience, and personality of the teacher are additional factors that enter into one's choice of methods.

Because of special talent, let's say of a dramatic nature, some teachers enjoy guiding pupils to play roles. Others, maybe beginning teachers, feel so awkward themselves in role-playing that their feeling of uneasiness carries over to their pupils. Probably a teacher of this type should not attempt that particular method until he has had more experience and until he and his pupils have had many opportunities to know and trust each other completely.

While a person's strong and weak qualifications enter in, a teacher should not let them limit him to teaching in the same way always. Just because a "good Bible scholar" knows biblical content, he is not justified in lecturing all the time.

III. METHODS EFFECTIVE WITH TEEN-AGERS

With these preliminary considerations behind us, now let's think particularly about methods that can be used with a typical Intermediate class, that is, with a small group (ranging from four to ten) of teen-age boys or girls, assembled in a relatively small classroom adjacent to other classes, for a period of thirty or forty minutes of Bible study.

Though the "typical" situation is limited by certain factors, some more than others, teachers are not limited to just one or two methods.

1. *Lecture*

Lecturing is effective with Intermediates under certain specific conditions *only:*

(1) *Must be brief.*—Because pupil participation is at a minimum when the teacher lectures, this method should be used for only a minute or two at the time. No teacher of Intermediates should think of using *the* lecture method, but he will likely use an element of lecture in almost every class session in order to pull together a discussion pupils have had or to give a bit of new information which pupils need then and there or to introduce a new idea for consideration. But sustained talking by the teacher should be limited to a few minutes or even seconds. Pity Intermediates who have to listen to their teachers talk for thirty minutes!

(2) *Must be well done.*—Pupils respond to the teacher who plans for them to participate. They want to participate; their mind-set is conditioned to doing something themselves. For that reason, the teacher who undertakes to talk (even for a brief while) must be capable of getting and holding their interest. Otherwise his effort will be useless. Effective lecturing requires a great deal of skill—more than most teachers have, in fact.

Because this method of teaching has been used so ineffectively, it has fallen somewhat into disrepute. But when properly used, it can create a learning situation. Listening and reacting mentally to ideas expressed in a lecture are types of participation that can result in a creative learning experience.

2. *Group Discussion*

Discussion is much more effective than lecturing with teen-agers. Instead of having one person pass ideas on to them (as in a lecture), pupils think for themselves and pool their ideas in a discussion. After hearing various facts, opinions, and reactions, they arrive at self-made decisions.

Problem-solving and panels, which could be considered as separate methods, may likewise be thought of as types of group discussion.

> Adolescents should be given critical problems which will bring them face to face with the hard surfaces and sharp corners called the facts of life. . . . Now is the time to introduce them to the practical difficulties that will confront them throughout their careers.[1]

But unless properly planned and directed, discussion may deteriorate into aimless talk or biased argument. In this kind of activity the teacher must be responsible for seeing that the subject to be discussed is clear. In order to participate intelligently, every member of the group should know the issue under consideration, should recognize the problem or obstacles involved, and should work toward possible solutions. At times the teacher will have to help the group realize how far they have progressed. By raising questions here and there, he can keep them moving toward the learning goal.

(1) *Example.*—In a lesson on "Being Christian at Home" the discussion method could be used profitably to get pupils to consider their personal responsibility for unhappy home situations. They would need to pool their ideas on (1) types or areas of conflict within families (such as parent-child, husband-wife, brother-sister, grandparent-grandchild), (2) causes of conflict within these areas (such as lack of understanding, selfishness, jealousy, lack of money, too small living space), and (3) possible solutions.

(2) *Example.*—Pupils themselves might select four of their class members to compose a panel to consider, in a lesson on Joseph's being carried into Egypt, whether liabilities (away from his family, a country boy in a large city in a strange land, no knowledge of the Egyptian language, among people who worshiped idols) outweighted assets (was young

and handsome, had a keen mind, had faith in God, was morally strong).

In a panel type of discussion, the teacher, who serves more or less as moderator, should see that pupils who are listeners get the benefit of the discussion, too. "Audience participation" is desirable in a situation of this type.

Group discussion may be used to help create a learning situation, to identify and interpret the biblical passage, or to help pupils relate the truth to themselves. When properly used, this method opens up excellent teaching opportunities.

3. *Illustration*

Think of the times your wandering mind has been called back to the sermon theme or lesson subject by a good story or illustration well told. This method is effective with all age groups, especially with teen-agers, because it helps them see the truth in action. Jesus used parables to illustrate principles, and teachers today will do well to use stories or incidents to illustrate moral and spiritual abstractions.

In order to be effective, illustrations should be *brief, relevant* to the lesson theme, and *well told*. A long, drawn-out rehashing of the biblical narrative (which pupils have already read as a part of their lesson study) does not meet the requirements mentioned in the preceding sentence.

Illustrations which teachers collect for themselves are likely to be much better than ones they will find in somebody's volume of "best illustrations." Magazines, newspapers, biographies, and observation provide good illustrations for the teacher alert enough to spot them.

Especially is this teaching technique effective in clarifying content and in helping pupils know how to apply the truth.

(1) *Example.*—In an Old Testament lesson featuring Elijah as a lone individual standing for God, this biographical illustration was effective in helping Intermediates see that

one person, even a very young one, can make a difference by taking a right stand:

"Hey, fellows! Here comes the old peddler. Let's have some fun!" The boys of the village rushed into the streets as the old Jewish peddler with his donkey cart came along. It was lots of fun to torment him. They hooted, jeered, and laughed, and some of the "braver" ones even tugged at his coat. Then one of the boys noticed something as the old man turned around. Instead of shaking his fist and shouting at the boys, he smiled at them.

That one boy never forgot that smile. The next time the peddler came down the village street with his donkey cart, this boy went up to him and stuck out his hand. They shook hands; then the boy walked along beside the donkey cart. The two chatted away like real friends.

But what about the other boys? The coming of the peddler had been their signal for fun. They stood aside, looking confused and surprised. This time no one poked fun at the old man or his new pal. The boys weren't afraid of the peddler, but his new pal could outfight any of them.

And the peddler's pal is someone you know well, but you don't think of him as a bright-eyed boy beside a Jewish peddler's donkey cart. You picture him as a tall, slightly stooped man with a large mustache. People come to him with sleeping sickness, jungle fever, and leprosy. The whole world knows him as Dr. Albert Schweitzer.[2]

(2) *Example.*—While studying "Justice to Minorities," Intermediates were helped by this incident reported in the press to realize how serious false assumptions can be:

One afternoon in the spring of 1951, three olive-skinned ladies wearing Oriental saris walked into a beautiful new branch department store in New Rochelle, a suburb of New York City. "Gypsies!" thought the cop standing on the corner. So he called to the police headquarters, and two detectives came out at once. Surely enough, there were the suspects— two in the gift department, and one looking at a spoon in the silverware department. In spite of their protests, the detectives took the ladies to the police station at once for fear they would shoplift something from the white American's store.

When the officers finally listened to the ladies, they found much to their amazement that the three beautifully dressed women were wives of delegates from Pakistan to the United Nations. The policeman's only defense (after the Pakistan delegation at United Nations demanded an official apology) was, "We thought they were gypsies, and gypsies do steal!"

4. Scripture Searching

Contrary to some teachers' ideas, using the Bible in class can be a fascinating, as well as a profitable, activity for Intermediates. Creative Bible activities will turn a listless class into a group of eager searchers for information if the activity is properly motivated.

(1) *Example.*—In studying Proverbs 23:29–35, let pupils (*a*) find six questions distillers and liquor salesmen would not like to answer; (*b*) identify a verse answering all six questions; (*c*) point out in another verse the truth about beverage alcohol; (*d*) give proof found in another verse that it is habit-forming; and (*e*) underscore good advice for young people to follow.

(2) *Example.*—Ask pupils to identify in Genesis 3:6 three kinds of temptation Eve experienced when she looked at the forbidden fruit.

(3) *Example.*—Isaiah 53 will be more meaningful to pupils who search for parallels between it and references in the Gospels to Christ. For instance:

JOHN 1:46: "Can there any good thing come out of Nazareth?"

"He shall grow up before him as a tender plant, and as a root out of a dry ground: he hath no form nor comeliness; and when we shall see him, there is no beauty that we should desire him" (Isa. 53:2).

LUKE 19:41: "When he was come near, he beheld the city, and wept over it."

"A man of sorrows, and acquainted with grief" (Isa. 53: 3).

MATTHEW 27:12–14: "When he was accused of the chief priests and elders, he answered nothing. Then said Pilate unto him, Hearest thou not how many things they witness against thee? And he answered him to never a word; insomuch that the governor marvelled greatly."

"He was oppressed, and he was afflicted, yet he opened not his mouth: he is brought as a lamb to the slaughter, and as a sheep before her shearers is dumb, so he openeth not his mouth" (Isa. 53:7).

5. *Question-Answer*

Probably the most frequently (but not necessarily the most effectively) used method is this one: questions and answers. It is popular with teachers because it gives them the feeling that they are getting pupil participation.

Good questions are a good teaching technique, but poor ones aren't. Questions designed to stimulate thought and to help pupils formulate decisions are teaching aids. But those that can be answered with a hurried yes or no or a bit of factual information may not contribute a thing to the learning process. There are times, of course, when a teacher does need to ascertain through questions what facts pupils do know in order to guide them to the next step. Questions should be planned with learning goals in mind, just as illustrations and problems and discussion are planned with outcomes in mind.

The questions which pupils ask teachers are a better indication of what pupils are thinking than are the questions teachers ask them.

(1) *Example.*—In a lesson based on Adam's and Eve's experience in Eden, this thoughtful question was asked by a young teen-ager: Since God is able to do whatever he wants to do, why didn't he keep Adam and Eve from sinning?

(2) *Example.*—In a unit on "Christian Principles of Social Justice," one lesson dealt with justice on a community or neighborhood level. The following questions got pupils enough involved that they wanted to see how their community measured up to the teachings in the Scriptures chosen for the day: What do you like about your community? What would a newcomer probably dislike about it?

(3) *Example.*—While studying what Baptists believe about baptism, pupils became very much interested in discussing these questions: If a person was immersed after making his profession of faith in a church of another denomination, why should he have to be baptized again before he can become a member of a Baptist church? Aside from the fact that Jesus himself was immersed, why isn't sprinkling or pouring as significant a form of baptism as immersion?

6. Assignment (*Research and Report*)

The learning process is not supposed to be confined to the classroom itself. Certain methods calling for out-of-class activities can provide enriching experiences for individuals who accept assignments and for other class members who hear and discuss reports given to the group.

Junior and senior high youngsters, who are accustomed to homework in secular school and who respect the teacher providing "ample intellectual fare," are capable of doing some good research in the area of Bible study.

Sometimes it will be necessary for teachers to help pupils locate resource materials needed to prepare an assignment or project. Teachers should be very careful to create a good opportunity for pupils to report on their findings.

(1) *Example.*—Older Intermediates, interested in knowing what people of other denominations think about such things as baptism and the Lord's Supper, can be asked to do research in those areas.

(2) *Example.*—In a lesson on citizenship responsibilities

of Christians, all pupils were asked to write, before coming to class, a short theme on this subject: "Indifference—a Threat to Freedom."

(3) *Example.*—While studying a unit on the Bible and the way it came to us in its present form, a class arranged an attractive exhibit of Bibles printed in different languages.

(4) *Example.*—A unit having a missions emphasis can be enriched by pupil research into these areas: the education and experience required of appointees by the Foreign Mission Board; types of work carried out under the auspices of the Foreign Mission Board; geographical areas where workers are especially needed at present.

7. *Buzz Session*

This method is much newer than lecturing or the question-answer way of teaching. But it has been in use long enough to prove that it can be an effective way for a group to work together.

The large group (in our case a class composed of, let us say, eight pupils) is divided into smaller subgroups. As few as two people can make up a buzz group in a class situation. All of the groups work on the same problem and then share their findings with the whole class.

The chief merit of a buzz group is this: It calls for maximum pupil initiative and participation. The groups are on their own for a given period of time, for five minutes or longer.

(1) *Example.*—During a class period when sixteen-year-olds were studying Jesus' experience with the Samaritan woman at the well, under the lesson title "Ignoring Prejudice to Give Life," the class was divided into buzz groups to spend five minutes finding what the following incident reveals about prejudice:

Years ago an Italian family, coming to the United States to live, settled in a small Southern town. The Italians could speak English very poorly, with an obvious accent. Many people in the community had difficulty in their business dealing with the Italian father in making him understand. Soon they decided that all Italians are dumb. The children in the town began calling the Italian children unkind names. Some of the poorer people, afraid of competition for their jobs, wanted to run the Italians away or to try to limit them to jobs they did not want for themselves. The few who tried to be friendly to the foreigners were severely criticized by their neighbors. Not until the next generation had grown up were the Italians treated decently by the people of the town.

(2) *Example.*—Fifteen-year-olds, while studying the meaning of church membership, worked in buzz sessions for a while trying to interpret sections of the church covenant.

(3) *Example.*—Buzz groups were once asked to formulate one question each on which they wanted help regarding life after death.

8. *Field Trip and Interview*

Though these two methods call for out-of-class activity, they are effective because they are based on firsthand experience. Both require careful preparation. A field trip often involves transportation, permission of parents, arrangements with the place or person to be visited, and so on. The interview should be planned for the convenience of the person being interviewed. The Intermediate who is to do the interviewing needs help in knowing how to conduct an interview and how to share the results of the experience with the class. But in spite of the trouble involved, both of these methods can result in real learning experiences.

(1) *Example.*—The worship practices mentioned in the Bible will be much more meaningful to a group of teen-agers who have visited a Jewish temple or synagogue and have seen scrolls and phylacteries and have witnessed a Jewish worship service for themselves.

(2) *Example*.—The cost of following Christ was impressed upon an Intermediate told in an interview with Missionary Charles Whitten in 1959: "It is not easy to be a Christian in Spain. When a person stands to his feet and says, 'I accept Jesus Christ as my Saviour,' you can be sure that he has counted the cost. If he is employed, he will likely lose his job; if he is a businessman, it is probable that his establishment will be boycotted. In many cases it means that he will be alienated from his own family. However, this year we have seen scores of people stand calmly with a heavenly radiance on their faces as they said, 'Today I take my stand with Jesus, so help me God.'"

9. *Audio-Visuals*

Since audio-visuals must always be combined with other methods, sometimes we do not think of this as a distinct method. That conception is good, for visuals should not be expected to do a teaching job by themselves.

Through discussion or a given set of questions or some other technique, Intermediates should be prepared to see and to evaluate motion pictures or filmstrips.

Maps, chalkboards, flat pictures, graphs, and objects, as well as projected materials, should be used as aids, not as an end in themselves. And they should be used when they can help achieve a learning goal, not as an entertainment feature or as an easy way out of preparing a lesson. Unless the media will give a true impression of the person or incident or thing portrayed, a visual should not be used.

But when visuals of a high quality have been chosen because they can help open up the way for learning and when their use has been planned for properly, they are an excellent means of stimulating imagination, of giving accurate impressions, of conveying knowledge, and of inspiring noble decisions.

(1) *Example*.—Tracing on a map the journey of Abraham

and his family as they left Chaldea, crossed over the Euphrates River, and moved down into Canaan can help teenagers appreciate his response to God's call when "he went out, not knowing whither he went" (Heb. 11:8).

Map studies will likewise enrich a study of the Exodus, of Jesus' ministry, and of Paul's missionary journeys.

(2) *Example.*—A flat picture (or a slide) of the tabernacle, of a Palestinian sheepfold, and of a flat-roofed house in Capernaum will enable pupils to understand better the ancient Hebrew sacrificial rites, Jesus' comparison of himself to the door, and the reason why a crippled man could be let down through a roof in order to get to Jesus.

(3) *Example.*—A fourteen-minute film, *A Faithful Witness,* based on the work of Philip as recorded in Acts, may be used as enrichment material in a character study of Philip or in a survey of the book of Acts or in a lesson emphasizing personal responsibility for witnessing to others about Christ.

10. *Role-playing*

This method, like buzz groups, is a relatively new way of helping pupils learn. It can be an effective method because it enables pupils to see a situation from the inside, that is, from the other person's point of view.

Role-playing always evolves around a problem, preferably involving just two people. The class discuss the situation so that the basis of conflict is clear and the characters involved are rather well defined. Pupils volunteer or are chosen to act out, without rehearsing, a situation. In order to be true to the character one is portraying, he has to try to put himself emotionally and mentally in the place of the person whose role is being played.

The portrayal should be very brief, based on a single incident. Other members of the class observe and then comment on the interpretation given and the solution suggested by the role players.

The purpose always is to create understanding, not to entertain.

(1) *Example.*—Without being sacrilegious, two pupils could act out the moment on Mount Moriah when Isaac realized that his father was ready to offer him as a sacrifice to Jehovah. One role-player would try to understand what went on in the heart and mind of this aged father (who had waited so long for a son) when he felt that God wanted him to offer that son on a burning altar. The other would try to put himself in the place of a trusting youth at the moment he realized what was about to happen.

(2) *Example.*—Role-playing is especially good in the area of application. In a lesson on "Why Be Honest?" three pairs of pupils role-played this situation:

A seven-year-old discovered to his delight that the neighborhood grocer had by mistake given him a dime in change instead of a penny. How could his fifteen-year-old brother best lead him to see the importance of returning the dime?

The first actor brother tried to do so by telling the child that to keep the dime would be stealing and that the law punishes people who steal. The second one threatened that God wouldn't love him if he broke one of the Commandments. The third playing the role, who the class felt offered the best solution to the problem, tried to help his little brother realize how he (the seven-year-old) would feel if he were in the place of the clerk who had made the mistake in giving change.

Variety of method will enrich the teaching-learning experience. But appropriateness is more important than variety. Regardless of how attractive a method may be, it is not appropriate for use in a Sunday school class if it merely entertains or if it manipulates pupils to answer without thinking. To be worthy of use, it must motivate the class to search for the revelation of God's will and to act in accordance with it.

FOR FURTHER CONSIDERATION

1. Look back over last Sunday's lesson and identify the methods suggested in the procedure. What additional ones did you use?
2. What success have you had with some of the newer methods, such as buzz groups, role-playing, and interview?
3. Share with the group an experience your class has had in effective Scripture searching.

---

[1] Gilbert Highet, *The Art of Teaching* (New York: Vintage Books, 1956), p. 152. Used by permission of Alfred A. Knopf, Inc.

[2] Wilbur Howard, "The Peddler's Pal," *Lessons for Intermediates,* The Methodist Publishing House, January–March, 1958. Used by permission.

CHAPTER 7

I. IMPERATIVE PRELIMINARIES
   1. Lesson Truth Summarized
   2. Learning Goals Stated

II. SUGGESTIONS FOR CREATING A LEARNING SITUATION
   1. Striking Statement, Quotation, or Question
   2. Pertinent Illustration
   3. Problem Presented
   4. Current Happenings

III. PLANS FOR DIRECTING PUPILS IN USING THE BIBLE

IV. PROCEDURE FOR HELPING PUPILS RELATE TRUTH TO THEMSELVES

7

The Weekly Teaching Plan

A WRITTEN PLAN is an aid in the teaching-learning process. The very discipline required to put a plan into writing forces the teacher to think more clearly and to plan more specifically than he would otherwise. So let's go on the assumption from this time on that every teacher will write out his teaching plan every week.

The teacher's lesson periodical provides aid in this very area. In addition to interpreting the message of the Scriptures, the lesson writer helps the teacher to know *how* to plan so that pupils will discover the biblical truth and will want to appropriate it to themselves.

Quite often extensive adaptations have to be made in the procedure suggestions as well as in the learning goals suggested in the quarterly in order for them to be as meaningful as possible for a particular class. The writer knows teen-agers in general but not the particular Jane or Bill. The given plan is meant to stimulate the thinking of the teacher and to offer guidance as he maps out his own procedure. The plan in the teacher book is not meant to be followed slavishly.

I. IMPERATIVE PRELIMINARIES

Working out the teaching plan is the culminating activity to a lot of preparation that has gone on before. At least four significant steps should precede this final one: mastering the biblical content, summarizing the biblical truth, considering pupil interests and needs related to this truth, and deciding upon learning goals.

It is a good idea to incorporate two of these features in the teaching plan itself. Having the summarizing truth and the learning goals directly before him will guide the teacher as he plans learning experiences for his class.

1. *Lesson Truth Summarized*

For instance, in a lesson on Jesus' friendship with the family at Bethany, the Scripture selections may point to this central truth: *When Christ is welcomed into a home, his presence enriches family relationships and provides family members a way to honor him.*

Thinking of various pupils in his class, the teacher may realize that Tom needs help in adjusting to his nervous, high-strung grandmother, who has recently come to live with his family. Luke's parents are divorced. If the class members are fifteen or sixteen, they may be thinking of getting married and establishing their own homes.

2. *Learning Goals Stated*

In view of such situations, what learning goal will the teacher decide upon? Possibly it may be stated thus: *to discover in Jesus' friendship with the Bethany friends what Jesus' presence can do to bless a home and how family members can honor him.*

With these two italicized features (summary truth and learning goal) written at the top of a sheet of paper, the teacher is ready to proceed with the making of his teaching plan.

II. SUGGESTIONS FOR CREATING A LEARNING SITUATION

The first classroom responsibility the teacher must plan for is the motivation of pupils so that they will want to learn. The motivating activity must be one that they can relate to themselves; pupils have to become involved in the situation personally. Otherwise nothing will happen on the inside.

(Remember the directives based on learning principles discussed in chapter 4.)

Let's consider some techniques for creating a good learning situation.

1. *Striking Statement, Quotation, or Question*

A thought-provoking question will often stimulate pupils to want to learn. In a lesson on the social responsibility of a Christian, a question of this type would motivate reaction: Why isn't drinking, especially social drinking, strictly a personal matter?

Intermediates will identify themselves immediately with this question: Why, do you suppose, are we often more considerate of people outside the family than we are of our own parents and brothers or sisters?

Their reaction to Robert Frost's definition of home given in "Death of the Hired Man" could be another approach to Bible study on family relations:

"Home is the place where, when you have to go there,
    They have to take you in." [1]

In a lesson having to do with the relationship of man to his fellow man, this statement made by a person who isn't an American should stimulate thoughtful discussion: "It is neither God nor the physical universe the American fears, since he sees himself as the associate of one and the master of the other. What he truly fears is his fellow man."

2. *Pertinent Illustration*

An incident or illustration can be used effectively to create a learning situation provided it is relevant to teen-age experience and to the biblical truth of the lesson.

This one, which motivated pupils for a lesson study on baptism, came from the experience of a missionary: Years ago in interior China a group of converts were eagerly awaiting the coming of the missionary to their village so that they might be baptized and become church members. His visits were infrequent because his area was quite large. His long-looked-for visit came, unfortunately, at a time of severe drought, when there was not enough water available for a baptismal service. The converts suggested a solution. They dug a grave, and the minister, standing in the empty grave, repeated the words of the baptismal service and lowered each convert and then raised him up again.

After hearing this illustration, pupils were asked whether they would have been satisfied had they been one of the converts. After considering the experience, they were ready to try to discover in the Bible the real meaning of baptism.

3. *Problem Presented*

A situation that challenges pupils to decide, What would you do in a case like this? is a good technique for motivating learning. This case from a teen-ager is an example:

"An old man in our neighborhood is just an old grouch. He is always tattling to our parents, sticking his nose in where it is none of his business. He has it in for us high school kids. He lives next door to me and is always yelling at us to get quiet if the gang drops by after a game to yak a while. Some of the boys have decided to get even with him on Halloween. They're going to trample down his flowers (he's nuts about them), paint up his car, and do some other damage. I've tried to talk them out of it, but they won't listen. Should I warn the old man, tell my folks, or just let human nature take its course? The fellows will really be mad at me if I tell."

This is another illustration of the same technique: Jim has been dedicated to the ministry since before his birth. His mother promised God that if he would give her a son, she would give him back to the Lord. Jim has known about his mother's vow all his life and has grown up with the idea of being a preacher. But now that he is in high school and is thinking seriously about his lifework, he doesn't feel that God is calling him to the ministry. He is a fine Christian boy and wants to do God's will. He also hates to disappoint his mother. What would you do if you were Jim?

4. *Current Happenings*

Most of us are more keenly interested in what is happening close around than we are in what has happened long ago or far away. So current incidents in such realms as athletics, politics, or school activities may be just the thing to use to get a class of teen-agers interested in studying the Bible. For instance:

Arthur, the neighborhood newsboy, reported with delight one night as he stopped by to collect for the paper: "We had a new experience at school today. Rosita Juarez, a Latin, enrolled, but we do not want any Latins at Hillsboro. Let her go back to West High, where her kind are. Do you know what we decided to do? Give her the silent treatment. Nobody's going to have anything to do with her. We are just going to freeze her out!"

Whatever the nature of the material used, the first step in a teaching plan must be worked out with this purpose in mind: *to get pupils so deeply involved that they will want to find an answer to their questions or a solution to their problems.*

III. PLANS FOR DIRECTING PUPILS IN USING THE BIBLE

The Bible is the source to which we turn to find answers to our questions and directions for our lives. In a sense this search into God's Word is the most important feature of any Sunday school class period. Plans must be carefully made for directing pupils in meaningful use of the Bible.

Experience proves that the reading of the Bible aloud by

the teacher or one of his pupils or letting each take turns at reading verses is not the best way to use the Bible. Let's note some better ways.

In a lesson designed to make young folk conscious of the quality of work God expects from each of us, one resourceful teacher led his pupils to construct from the given Scripture references an ad such as appears in the "Help Wanted" section of a daily paper. Pupils searched the various passages for a specific purpose, namely, looking for qualities pleasing to God. This was the outcome of the Bible activity:

"HELP WANTED: Young boy [girl], age _____, willing to give a full week's work; Sundays off [Ex. 20:9–10]. Must have purpose and goal in life but be ready to work hard at present task [Eccl. 9:10]. Must be honest, produce good work, and be unselfish [Eph. 4:28]; willing to take orders and carry out duty with sincerity, heartiness, and conviction. Applicant must realize that all work is for the glory of God [Col. 3:22–24] and that any failures or inefficiencies will be dealt with on equal basis for all employees [Col. 3:25]. Salary is good, benefits are plentiful, and management is fair and considerate [Col. 4:1]."

Some younger Intermediates might find that particular activity too difficult, but they would not find it too difficult to decide, for instance, why Deuteronomy 15:7–8 would be a good passage for a Community Chest or United Givers Fund solicitor to know. They could easily contrast the command God gave Adam and Eve (Gen. 2:15–16) with Satan's interpretation of it (Gen. 3:1).

Two good readers, one taking the part of Eve and the other the part of Satan, could make the dialogue in Genesis 3 come alive. The same technique (dramatic reading) could be used in the conversations of God and Satan as recorded in the opening chapters of Job.

Words underscored, comments written in the margin, and

occasional reading in concert are other ways for pupils to use their Bibles.

Good resource material is available in every lesson development in the teacher books to help teachers work out step 2 in the teaching plan, namely, *ways to direct pupils to do purposeful Bible study.*

The Scripture searching activity is not an end in itself, and it should not be the final feature of the class period. But it is an important one, and plenty of time should be devoted to it.

IV. PROCEDURE FOR HELPING PUPILS RELATE THE TRUTH TO THEMSELVES

If the Bible activities aren't to be the climax of a class period, what should be? *The decisions pupils themselves make as an outgrowth of the truth they have found in God's Word.* These decisions will determine the change or growth, as talked about in the very first chapter.

A teacher should plan as carefully for this portion of the class period as for other features. Unless he does plan this step, he will likely do a little moralizing, and his pupils will likely walk out of the classroom and forget what their teacher has said.

Some of the same types of methods used to create a learning situation at the beginning of the class session can be used here to motivate pupils to put their newly found knowledge or understanding to work in their lives day by day.

An illustration of sacrificial giving may inspire a teen-age girl to do without something she really wants in order to make a contribution to her church.

A statement such as this one by a Moslem father may challenge a boy to evaluate his own influence: "I am a Moslem and will always remain one. But if my son chooses to be a Christian, then teach him to be a good one."

Problem-solving and case studies may be used effectively to help pupils decide what they should do. For instance, in a lesson on Esther, the purpose of which is *to help pupils recognize the need today for courageous people who will stand for the right, even at great risk,* the class may be challenged to accept responsibility by considering this question: How would you feel toward Esther, or any other Jew, who denied her heritage in order to gain favor of some sort? What about a Christian who refuses to take a stand in defense of some Christian principle because he is afraid of losing out with the crowd?

The teacher should check this part of his plan against the learning goals stated at the top of his sheet. The two should be very closely related.

With pupil and teacher books as aids and with the Holy Spirit as counsellor and guide, any teacher who is willing to work can learn how to make plans which will enable him to do an effective job of teaching.

FOR FURTHER CONSIDERATION

1. Is there any conflict between a teacher's plan to motivate learning and the concept that genuine learning must be self-motivated?
2. What technique did you use last Sunday to create a favorable learning situation?
3. Suggest advantages current illustrations have over "canned" ones.
4. What methods are particularly good for helping pupils relate biblical truth to themselves?
5. As a group activity, prepare a work sheet similar to the one illustrated and use it as a guide in evaluating the pupil participation which may be expected to result, in an Intermediate class, from the use of the teaching methods listed.

TEACHING METHODS AND PUPIL PARTICIPATION

Teaching Method	Degree of Pupil Participation		Types of Pupil Participation	Appropriate for What Age Group(s)
	Maximum	Minimum		
Story				
Illustration (modified story)				
Discussion				
Guided Conversation (modified discussion)				
Question-and-answer				
Lecture				
Bible Searching				
Project				
Visual				
Dramatic				

[1] Frost, *Come In and Other Poems* (New York: Henry Holt and Company, Inc., 1943), p. 115. Used by permission of publishers.

CHAPTER 8

I. PRELUDE TO THE LESSON

   1. The Assembly, a Learning Opportunity
   2. Records Also Teach
   3. Officers Learn by Doing

II. PREVIOUS WEEKDAY PREPARATION FOR A LESSON

   1. Biblical Content Studied
   2. Truth Summarized
   3. Pupil Needs and Interests Considered
   4. Learning Goal Established

III. THE TEACHING PLAN

   1. Creating a Learning Situation
   2. Searching God's Word
   3. Relating the Lesson to Individual Life Needs

8

On Sunday Morning

In the experience of a Sunday school teacher, Sunday morning is a climactic time. His various efforts have been expended in anticipation of the thirty-five or forty-minute period he will spend with his class. So let's think about these moments when teachers and pupils work together.

I. Prelude to the Lesson

In addition to the class sessions, there are other teaching-learning activities on Sunday morning.

1. *The Assembly, a Learning Opportunity*

Ordinarily a feature which we call an assembly precedes the class period. In a Sunday school having separate departments for various age groups, Intermediates meet together for fifteen or twenty minutes in a department room before going into the class session. In nondepartment schools, they usually assemble with Young People and Adults for a short while. This period, under the direction of the department superintendent (the general superintendent in a class Sunday school), is another learning opportunity pupils have, though not one for which the teacher is responsible.

Often the purpose of this period is to create a worship situation so that pupils will be in a "spiritual frame of mind" as they enter into their class activities. Well-chosen themes, developed through appropriate music, Scripture selections, prayers, and other features, can help teen-agers realize that they are in the Lord's house on the Lord's Day for the purpose of studying his Word.

A program for this purpose must, however, be more than "a sweet little devotional" brought by someone. It should be a carefully planned session designed to help workers and pupils draw close to God in spirit so that he can make known his will through Bible study.

At other times this assembly period will be used to develop some character-building theme or to acquaint Intermediates with some denominational need or emphasis. It may be devoted sometimes to the consideration of personal problems youngsters face, with the purpose, of course, of helping them work out a satisfactory solution.

This assembly can be, and will be if properly planned, a very significant session. But it is just a prelude to the more important one, namely, the class period. For that reason department superintendents should plan programs that will come well within the allotted time.

Each assembly program should be planned with the needs of particular Intermediates in mind. Suggested programs are offered in *The Sunday School Builder* and in the superintendent's books in the Cycle Graded series.

2. Records Also Teach

Probably the heading should read "Records Teach What?" for in many instances class records are made up and are promoted in such a way that they teach wrong values instead of right ones. The Six Point Record System was never meant to be an end in itself. When so much emphasis is put on grades that a pupil marks his lesson studied though he has merely glanced at a paragraph or two, the record system is being abused.

But when properly interpreted and when conscientiously met, the six points involved help pupils to grow in character, as well as to improve the quality of the Bible study they do.

Records should be compiled efficiently so that the process will not consume time needed for lesson study.

3. *Officers Learn by Doing*

The importance of pupil activity is stressed throughout this book. But the brief class period on Sunday morning is not the time for class officers to go into a lot of detailed business. The monthly meeting is the time for details. The class president and other officers should be trained to function quickly and efficiently in order to leave full time for Bible study. For instance, a long harangue over a proposed class party can completely destroy the spirit of worship created during the assembly and can make it difficult for pupils to get back into a learning mood.

These comments are not meant to minimize the importance of class officers. They are meant, instead, to encourage teachers to see that the officers function efficiently.

II. Previous Weekday Preparation for a Lesson

Though an earlier chapter (chap. 5) discussed lesson preparation in detail, let's think once again about effective preparation. In order to be practical, let's take one specific lesson and go through the entire process. If you prefer (and if your conference leader agrees), you may work on next Sunday's lesson instead of the one suggested here. But be sure that you follow the same procedure.

Let us assume that we have a given subject—"The Forgiving Father"—based on the parable of the prodigal son, recorded in Luke 15 : 11–32.

First must come the four steps in preparation (mastering biblical content, summarizing the lesson truth, considering pupil needs and interests, deciding upon learning goals), climaxed by the fifth—working out a teaching plan.

1. *Biblical Content Studied*

Jesus' public ministry was drawing to a close. The opposition of the scribes and Pharisees was so strong that the Master withdrew with his disciples for two or three months into Perea, across the Jordan River from Palestine proper. During that time came the attack which called forth this parable from Jesus. The fact that Jesus talked with sinners, even ate with them, was more than the strict religionists could stand. There was burning hatred in their voices as they whispered, "This man receiveth sinners, and eateth with them."

A family situation.—The parables of Jesus were specific enough to be realistic, but they were also general enough for the message to be applied to varying individuals and situations. For instance, we are told no details about the family in the parable except that "a certain man had two sons." Family stories had an appeal then, as now. The publicans (tax collectors) and sinners who had drawn near to hear Jesus (Luke 15:1) were, or at least had been, members of some family. Maybe this opening sentence called to their minds experiences of some days that they had almost forgotten.

The murmuring scribes and Pharisees in the crowd (Luke 15:2) may have listened with a little more sympathy when Jesus started talking about a father who had two sons. No doubt their ire was up again, though, by the time he had finished his story, for the last part was a definite condemnation of their very attitudes.

No details are given to suggest what provoked the younger son to ask for his inheritance. The absence of details would suggest, however, that there had been no upheaval within the family. Probably his request was unusual (ordinarily heirs came into their inheritance when the father died), but the younger son did not ask that partiality be shown. Instead, he requested that part which fell to him. According to the

Mosaic law recorded in Deuteronomy 21:16-17, the older son (the first-born) received double the amount the other heirs received. The older son in this story received his double share of the property at the same time the younger son received his portion.

A family crisis.—An unannounced plan must have been developing in the younger son's mind, even at the time he asked for his inheritance. Likely he had grown restless on his father's estate. He wanted his freedom. Gaining financial independence was the first step; leaving home was the second.

An understanding of the reactions of the various persons involved was left to the imagination of the listeners to whom Jesus was talking. The story will be more meaningful to the reader who thinks about this father and two sons long enough to decide how each must have felt on this occasion.

No doubt each sensed it to be significant. Until this time, the three had lived together and had worked side by side. The younger's decision would change that pattern. Whatever his reason, he wanted to leave; otherwise he would have continued living in his father's household.

The lure of the distant city offered greater thrills than the familiar family routine. In a distant place the young man would be free to do as he pleased. No longer would he be under the watchful eye of his father or older brother. His decision was self-centered, without question. Anticipation and excitement, probably sobered somewhat by the reality of leaving home for the first time, undoubtedly dominated the farewell scene as far as the younger son was concerned.

What about the father's reaction? Maybe he was hurt to think that his son wanted to leave. Or he may have thought philosophically that it was natural for youth to want independence. Regardless of how he felt personally, he recognized his son's right to choose for himself, and at the same time he must have recognized the wilfulness of the boy's choice. Yet he did not try to force him to stay against his will.

Later action indicates, however, that the father must have been anxious the day he told his son good-by.

The older brother may not have been grieved at all. He may have been jealous of one daring enough to seek a new kind of life. Or he may have been relieved to see his younger brother go, thinking that he would not have to compete with him thereafter.

The record simply says, "Before very long [that is, soon after receiving his inheritance], the younger son collected all his belongings and went off to a foreign land" (Phillips).[1]

A moral crisis.—The son fled from home in order to be free of parental influence, but soon he was in bondage. Just what downward steps he took we do not know. We can imagine, however, for the words "wasted" and "riotous" (or wild extravagance) give some idea. Frequently he is pictured as having lived the life of a real reprobate. The brother's accusation, which may not have been true, that he wasted his money on harlots, has been the basis for much conjecture.

We do not know what place Jesus had in mind when he used the term "far country." Jews from Palestine were settled at that time in such cities as Alexandria in Egypt, Tarsus in Asia Minor, or Rome in faraway Italy. The young man may have gone to one of these places, any one of which had facilities for leading a person into a life of extravagance and sin. Whatever the son did, the implication is quite clear that his activities in the distant country fell far below accepted moral standards. His effort to be free made him a servant of sin.

An economic crisis.—Probably this young man planned to settle down after having a good time on the money he had received from his father. But before he regained his squandered fortune, famine struck, and "he began to be in want."

We know that work was scarce, for otherwise a Jew would never have taken a job tending swine. From the earliest days of the Mosaic law, Hebrews had considered hogs unfit for food, and a social curse was put upon a Jew who kept them. In the thinking of the people in Jesus' audience that day, this young fellow could not have brought greater disgrace upon himself or his family than by working as a swineherd.

The job, strange to say, did not even pay enough for him to buy decent food. He who ordinarily would have scorned to eat pork was forced to eat food provided by the owner for the hogs. The pod of carob beans (similar to locust pods) was commonly used as fodder.

A *moral victory*.—In the midst of filth, rags, shame, and hunger the young man came to his senses. He thought of the food in his father's house, while he was dying of hunger. He who had revolted against obedience suddenly faced up to the ruin brought about by his wilfulness.

Instead of just feeling sorry for himself, he became ashamed of himself and of the mess he had made of his life. Recognition of his defilement was the first step in his conversion experience. But he didn't stop there. His conscience stirred him to act. With a new purpose in life he said, "I will arise and go to my father, and will say unto him, Father, I have sinned against heaven, and before thee."

Whereas before he had said, "Give," this time he would pray his father to let him be a servant. He was willing to accept any position just so long as he was back in the secure fold of his home.

A *happy welcome*.—The moral victory was won that day in the pigpen, but the young man still faced difficulty. The journey home had just begun. He was still dirty and ragged and hungry. He still had to face his father and admit that he had thrown away his inheritance entrusted to him. The neighbors and friends and relatives would still remember the news that had drifted back about his wild life in the city. Even if his father forgave him and let him work as a hired servant on the farm, there would still be serious consequences to face, but he was willing at last to face them.

The experience ended happily because of the character of the father. The old man had not given up hope of his son's return. He must have watched and prayed daily for him. Then upon his return, instead of reprimanding him for his wilfulness, the father did not let the returned boy finish his confession. He heard enough to know that his son had come home in a spirit of deep humility, repentant for the way he had done and willing to bear the consequences if only his father would forgive him.

As a token of his forgiveness, the father gave hurried orders for a feast to be prepared, for the returned prodigal to be clothed in garments befitting an honored guest, and for the neighbors to be invited in to rejoice over the son who was as dead but had come alive. Giving him the ring was the climax of the father's welcome, for it denoted the boy's restoration to the rank of sonship and freedom.

The presence of the Pharisees.—The Pharisees, Jesus' enemies, were present at the prodigal's return in the person of the older brother. He reproached his father for restoring the younger brother to the good graces of the family after his escapades in the far country. The father was not partial to either boy. He loved the younger and had longed for his return, but he also appreciated the loyalty and dependability of the older son.

The Pharisees reprimanded Jesus for receiving sinners into his fellowship. But God's love was great enough to include Pharisees and publicans and sinners. God would not, however, force his love and blessings upon either. Both were being bestowed upon all who came to Jesus in true repentance seeking salvation.

2. *Truth Summarized*

God is eager to forgive anyone who repents of his sin and turns to him for salvation, regardless of his past.

3. *Pupil Needs and Interests Considered*

[Just as we have assumed a given lesson subject and passage, let's assume a given class of fifteen-year-old girls.]

All of the group are professing Christians. [That fact is significant, for it helps determine the learning goal.] Being from upper middle class families, they have financial and educational advantages. Furthermore, they have "grown up in the church" and still attend Sunday school and the morning worship service regularly. Three of the group do not participate in any other church organizations, however.

These girls will be able to identify themselves somewhat with the younger son in the parable, for they want freedom from parental authority. While their desire for independence is a natural one and signs of it are wholesome, Jane's rebellion against her father's discipline and Lou's antagonistic feeling toward her mother are signs of unwholesome attitudes.

Polly is proud of her family money and tries to use it as a means of exerting pressure on the other girls. All of them are wrapped up in social activities and want prestige.

All except Mary acted snobbish when a girl from Mulberry Street Mission visited the class a few weeks ago and suggested that she might start coming to our church instead of going to the mission. Later they said that they did not want a girl of that type in the class because they did not want to have to include her in weekday class activities.

The girls are not soul-winners. They show no real concern for lost people in our town or for the cause of foreign missions. Though they are spending a lot of money on Christmas gifts for each other, they gave only dimes and quarters to the Lottie Moon Christmas Offering last Sunday.

4. *Learning Goal Established*

Based on the needs and interests of these girls, the teaching goal may be *to lead pupils to compare their attitude toward the lost or spiritually weak with God's attitude as portrayed by the father in the parable of the prodigal son.*

III. The Teaching Plan

[At last the time has come, in our imagination, for us to teach the Sunday school lesson. The assembly is over; the records have been made; and the president has turned the class over to the teacher. Now what? From this point on, suggestions will be given in the form of directives to teachers.]

1. *Creating a Learning Situation*

You may begin by proposing this question: Suppose you were a parent. What acts or attitudes do you think you would find hard to forgive in a son or daughter? [*Group discussion*] Without attracting special attention, jot answers on the board as pupils express themselves.

When you feel that they have become sufficiently involved in the question, suggest that they will want to measure their personal feelings by the attitude and action of a father and an older brother in a parable Jesus once used. [*Transition to next step*]

2. *Searching God's Word*

Explain briefly to the class that this incident took place late in Jesus' ministry, when the opposition of the scribes and Pharisees had become very strong. [*Lecture*]

After they have turned in their Bibles to Luke 15, ask pupils to identify the speaker and the audience mentioned in verses 1-2. [*Scripture searching*] Then raise this question: What about the relation of scribes and Pharisees to publicans and sinners? [*Question-answer*]

Have someone read from verse 2 the criticism which caused Jesus to tell this story, known as the parable of the prodigal son. Ask all to underscore in verse 10 a truth Jesus wanted to emphasize. [*Scripture searching*]

In preparation for discussion, ask all to read silently Luke 15:11-12. Explain that ordinarily in a Jewish family sons inherited their share of the estate when the father died, not before. [*Lecture or report* if assignment has been made in advance to look up inheritance practices.]

Then ask: What reasons, do you think, did the young man have for asking for his inheritance? [*Question-answer*]

As pupils look at a map, let two or three volunteers point out distant places where he might have gone. [*Visual*] Then let them find in verses 13 and 30 clues as to what he did in the foreign city. [*Scripture searching*]

After they have read verses 14-16, ask someone to point out details showing how desperate the young man became. [*Scripture searching*] Have another to read the realization he came to in verse 17 and someone else to read his resolution in verses 18-19. [*Scripture searching*]

After each pupil has read for himself the description of the reunion in verses 20-24, direct the group to consider two questions: What sins did the father have to forgive in his son? (List on the board the answers, which will include such as, squandered his fortune, disgraced the family name, caused his father to worry.) Why was it not hard for the father to forgive him? (The son really repented and wanted to make restitution; the father's love was so great, etc.) [*Group discussion*]

If it seems wise, let two volunteers act out the scene of reunion. [*Role-playing*]

Ask pupils to look for, as you read aloud verses 25-32, contrasts between the reunion of the younger son and his father and the scene that took place between the older son and the father. [*Scripture searching*] If time permits, this incident might also be acted out. [*Role-playing*]

Let the group suggest sins the older son was guilty of (list parallel with younger son's), the father's attitude toward him, and the older son's situation at the end of the story. (Be sure that pupils recognize his unrepentant attitude and his indifference toward his brother's salvation, as well as his selfishness and stubbornness.) [*Group discussion*]

3. *Relating the Lesson to Individual Life Needs*

Let pupils identify the persons represented by the characters in the story. Then ask: Who are modern publicans? Who are modern Pharisees? [*Question-answer*]

Call attention to the first list written on the board of things pupils find hard to forgive in others. Ask each to measure her own attitude toward forgiveness by God's willingness to forgive as revealed in the parable. Call attention to the second and third columns (younger and older brothers' sins), and ask each to search her own heart and to acknowledge silently ways in which she is disappointing God.

Though response should be entirely voluntary, create the opportunity for letting the class share their realizations and resolutions. If they really want to do something as an outcome of this learning experience, the Lottie Moon Christmas Offering and the girl from Mulberry Street Mission are two possibilities for consideration.

FOR FURTHER CONSIDERATION

1. In what ways can teachers and the superintendent co-operate to make the assembly period a meaningful experience for all? Recall a recent assembly program in your department (a general assembly, if your school does not provide a separate Intermediate department). Which of the four purposes presented on pages 97–98 would you say was dominant in the assembly? Do you believe the assembly was actually "a learning opportunity"?
2. What values should pupils learn from the Six Point Record System?
3. Where in this given lesson plan might other methods have been used? Which ones?

4. The study of this chapter has been profitable to you if it has guided you in building a lesson plan for a specific lesson. Which of the methods which have been considered have you included in your plan? What pupil activities do you expect will result if you follow the plan you have made? What visual aids will you use during the teaching procedure?
5. Show how a teacher might use the Lottie Moon Christmas Offering in leading pupils to do something as an outcome of their learning experience in the lesson discussed in this chapter. What opportunity for relating the lesson to individual needs do you see in the class attitude toward the girl from Mulberry Street Mission?

---

[1] J. B. Phillips, *The New Testament in Modern English* (New York: The Macmillan Co., copyright 1958 by J. B. Phillips), p. 158. Used by permission.

CHAPTER 9

I. ENLISTMENT OF FAMILY CO-OPERATION
  1. Through Parent-Worker Meetings
  2. Through Visitation

II. CO-ORDINATION OF YOUTH ACTIVITIES

III. WEEKLY TEACHING IMPROVEMENT PERIOD

IV. PARTICIPATION IN DENOMINATIONAL TEACHING-TRAINING ACTIVITIES
  1. Church Study Course for Teaching and Training
  2. Assemblies
  3. Clinics

V. THE TEACHER'S COUNSELING ROLE

VI. EMPHASIS ON GROUP DYNAMICS

VII. EVALUATION OF TEACHING
  1. Pupil Reaction
  2. Knowledge Acquired
  3. Inward Changes

9

Some Current Trends

ONE THING I do, forgetting what lies behind and straining forward to what lies ahead, I press on toward the goal for the prize of the upward call of God in Christ Jesus. Let those of us who are mature be thus minded; and if in anything you are otherwise minded, God will reveal that also to you. Only let us hold true to what we have attained" (Phil. 3:13–16 RSV).

A teacher in a Baptist Sunday school must hold true to the basic theological beliefs of Baptists. Otherwise, he is not worthy to hold office in a Baptist organization. At the same time, every teacher should grasp new ideas which will enable him to be a better steward of the "upward call of God in Christ Jesus."

Let us consider a few relatively new developments taking place in the area of Christian education, some of which first received emphasis in secular education or in the undertakings of other denominations.

I. ENLISTMENT OF FAMILY CO-OPERATION

Though teachers in Baptist Sunday schools have for a long time expressed verbally the importance of parental influence and of family life, we have been rather slow to enlist the co-operation of parents in our Bible teaching endeavors. Parents, on the other hand, have all too often been glad to let the church assume full responsibility for the religious training of children.

At last Sunday school teachers have acknowledged that

we cannot do the job alone, for "the wellspring of an integrated, healthy and happy personality lies within the walls—large or small, many or few, bare, painted or tapestried—of the teenager's home." [1]

Conscientious parents are likewise beginning to realize more than before that they cannot delegate to another their God-given responsibility of religious teaching and training.

> Parents' values are of crucial importance. The parent who has high standards and values and lives by them is a reservoir of strength to the adolescent confronted with conflicting standards and practices. [2]

So a great deal of thought is being given to ways Sunday school teachers and parents can work together to help teenagers achieve spiritual maturity commensurate with their years. Churches are trying to help parents discover good ways for giving their adolescent sons and daughters a chance to think, explore, and express themselves so that they may know what they believe and why and what they are willing to stand for. In an earlier chapter the teacher's responsibility was described as bringing "individuals into the vicinity where God himself may speak through the Bible." Parents should consider it their privilege and responsibility to build the kind of home where God can speak through daily relationships and activities.

Statistics verify the fact that many families need help in such an undertaking. One mother out of five works outside the home. According to recent census findings, between a third and a fourth of all teen-agers live in homes broken by divorce or death or some other cause. The increase in mental illness and in the crime rate of adolescents is outward evidence that many young people are not attaining the developmental goals discussed in chapter 3. Families, churches, and schools must work as a team to help them.

Let us think of ways in which parents and Sunday school teachers may share this mutual responsibility.

1. *Through Parent-Worker Meetings*

Certainly getting parents and Sunday school workers together once a year or quarterly or monthly will not solve all problems. But such meetings are a start in the right direction.

(1) *Purposes.*—Parent-worker meetings are good because of the purposes they can achieve.

In the first place, these occasions provide an opportunity for teachers and parents to meet each other (maybe for the first time in large churches). Even in one meeting it is possible for a friendly relationship to be established between a teen-ager's dad and his Sunday school teacher. Once such a relationship is established, it is then possible for parents to grow in appreciation of what the Sunday school is trying to do for a child and of what they can do to help. Parents, on the other hand, can give a teacher insight into the pupil's interests and needs that he could not discover by himself in a long time. Since teachers can be more objective than parents can be about their own children, they may, in turn, help a father and mother understand why their son or daughter behaves as he does.

These two groups can plan together how to make the home and church and community contribute to an Intermediate's best development.

(2) *Types of meetings.*—The purpose of a meeting (based on the needs of the ones involved) will to a large degree determine the nature of the meeting. Each of the following types has merit enough to warrant consideration. A fellowship or social period preceding or following always adds to the effectiveness of a parent-worker get-together.

a. Reproduction of the regular Sunday school department and class activities.—To parents who have never been in the youth area of the church or who do not know the kind of procedure followed, a meeting of this type would help interpret the activities their youngsters are engaged in on

Sunday morning. They would also have an opportunity to meet the teachers and to see them in action.

Parents should be encouraged to react to what they see. The Intermediates should probably not be present during the evaluation period.

b. Study groups.—Many parents who have not had an opportunity to study adolescent psychology (at least not recently) and who lack the initiative or materials to do serious reading of this nature will welcome an opportunity to study present-day teeners under the direction of a Christian leader. After one such study session, the mother of a sixteen-year-old said, "I wish I had heard all this four years ago. Bill has been a perfectly normal adolescent all the time, and I just didn't know it."

Sections of some current magazines designed for parents (*Home Life,* for instance) and books (such as *The Adolescent Views Himself, The American Teenager,* and *Youth: the Years from Ten to Sixteen,* quoted in preceding discussions) provide good resource material for parents and workers who need to understand more about teen-age development, interests, and problems. Church librarians, as well as workers in many public libraries, will be glad to help the leader or committee map out a study plan for as many sessions as seem wise.

The Family Life Department of the Baptist Sunday School Board will, as time goes by, have resource materials to make available or to recommend.

c. Discussion sessions.—Some parents who cannot or will not participate in regular study groups will respond with enthusiasm to an occasional opportunity to discuss their problems with other parents. Panels, made up of parents or of resource people (such as a doctor, a psychologist, a social worker, a church-related youth director) or of Intermediates themselves, can be very helpful in giving information about Intermediates or in analyzing their personal problems.

Parents, when properly motivated, will enjoy role-playing or buzz groups just as much as teen-agers. For instance, to consider the problems some parents have in talking things over with adolescents, the large group could be divided into buzz groups to analyze the following testimony of a teen-age boy for the purpose of discovering *why* the relationship is sometimes strained between parent and child:

> He wants me to lay the cards on the table, but when I ask him to, he just gets sore. You see, he can get sore because he's my father . . . you have to have respect—but sometimes he gets me so mad, when you know you're right and you know he's wrong, but he won't admit it. And he's trying to teach me to be a good sport. But boy, when I find that he's not a good sport. . . . Like last night he said, "I'll show you who's the master of this house." Master! As though this was the South and I'm a slave to him. That's what gets me mad. I'm no slave. He's my father . . . sometimes I talk to him for a while and he just says, "Yeah," and he doesn't talk with me. If he talked with me I'd feel great. If I keep talkin' for a while he says, "Can't you think of somethin' else besides that?" That's what gets me mad.[3]

Carefully selected films may be used as a springboard for a discussion of teen-age problems or of parental responsibility for Christian teaching and training. Consult the current issue of the *Baptist Book Store Catalog* for listing and description of projected audio-visual materials.

Though planning and promoting parent-worker meetings on a department basis is the responsibility of the administration, two things are sure: Teacher co-operation is necessary for the success of the meeting, and teachers can certainly receive as much benefit from the meetings as anyone else.

2. Through Visitation

For a long time the importance of visitation has been recognized for promotional purposes, especially the enlistment of new members and contacts with absentees. But visitation can likewise be so important in enlisting family co-operation that if the Sunday school teacher were limited to just one way of securing it, visitation would doubtless be the best choice.

Through a visit the teacher can sense, as well as hear from parents, conditions in the home that affect a pupil's attitude toward his peers, his teachers, his church, and even toward God. A quiet visit may be just the opportunity a mother has been waiting for to discuss some attitude or problem of her daughter. A visit may open up a chance for a teacher to share with a father the deep concern he feels about his son's apparent indifference toward church activities. A visit in the home is a good time to pray with a lost parent or Intermediate and try to win him to Christ. It is also a good time to acquaint parents with the lesson unit purpose and to seek their co-operation in helping make the biblical material meaningful.

Whereas a visit lacks the stimulus that comes from a large group thinking and planning together, it does provide opportunities for a closer relationship to develop between teacher and parent. Both meetings and visits can be used to strengthen the co-operative effort of individuals (parents and teacher) and of institutions (home and church) responsible for the Christian teaching and training of Intermediates.

II. Co-ordination of Youth Activities

Wholesome competition is good, but rivalry between youth organizations in a church is *not* good. The Sunday school alone cannot do as good job of stimulating and directing the spiritual growth of Intermediates as all organizations combined can do. The Sunday school class and department, the Intermediate union, the youth choir, the missionary organizations—each has a distinct contribution to make in attaining the objectives outlined in the first chapter. And workers in the various organizations should understand

and appreciate the responsibility and effort of their fellow workers in other types of youth activities.

A spirit of co-operation exists between the various age-group workers at your denominational headquarters. Curriculum materials are planned from a co-operative point of view so that each organization will carry its part of the load but will, at the same time, be duly appreciative of others who are bearing other aspects of responsibility.

Many churches are employing directors of youth activities, whose chief responsibility is to correlate and supervise work being done with and for teen-agers in the church. Schools of religious education in our seminaries are training young people for this particular vocation. Sunday school teachers have a vital part in furthering this ministry to youth by co-operating with all youth leadership in the church.

III. WEEKLY TEACHING IMPROVEMENT PERIOD

The idea of the weekly officers and teachers' meeting is certainly not new. But the idea of combining a study of biblical content with the theory of educational principles and an on-the-spot application of those principles is relatively new.

The purpose of the midweek coming together of Sunday school workers, either on a churchwide or a department basis, is no longer limited to considering promotional problems and hearing someone "teach" next Sunday's lesson. Instead, where meetings are most successful in terms of attendance and of help received, the purpose is to help teachers improve the quality of the teaching they are doing Sunday after Sunday.

With the needs of specific teachers in mind, superintendents sometimes plan for Bible content (included in the current unit of lessons or closely correlated to it) to receive major consideration. This purpose is worthy because teachers need to acquire a deeper understanding and appreciation of the Scriptures that will overflow into their teaching.

At other times special attention is focused on understanding age-group characteristics, problems, and needs (such as those discussed in this book and in other books in the teaching and training series).

An understanding of teaching and of teaching-learning principles is another area to be studied by Sunday school workers. Invariably where response to the weekly meeting is best, a workshop approach is being used. That is, after consideration has been given to biblical content or to theory, time is allowed for teachers to see how (or whether) the learning could (or should) be applied to the lesson to be taught next Sunday. There is also a close relationship between teacher interest in the meeting and teacher activity during the period. Teachers, like their pupils, learn best through meaningful participation.

Since the superintendent (general or department) is responsible for planning the teaching improvement period, no further details will be given in this discussion. But teachers, who will receive the greatest blessing from a good weekly meeting, must encourage and assist the administration in planning for it and in carrying out the plans effectively.

Further help in this particular area can be found in such books as *Building a Better Sunday School Through the Weekly Officers and Teachers' Meeting* by Gaines S. Dobbins, *Teaching for Results* and *Helping the Teacher* by Findley B. Edge. *The Sunday School Builder* (the monthly promotional magazine issued by the Sunday School Department of the Baptist Sunday School Board) includes in every issue suggestions to help build and maintain a strong midweek session designed to improve teaching.

IV. PARTICIPATION IN DENOMINATIONAL TEACHING-TRAINING ACTIVITIES

Southern Baptists are taking more seriously than ever before Paul's command to study in order to be unashamed workmen (2 Tim. 2:15). State and Convention-wide agencies are trying to reinforce the work that is being done on the local church level to improve the quality of teaching.

1. Church Study Course

This outlined course is meant as a guide for group or individual study. For the convenience of workers, various categories have been included in the course so that a proper balance may be kept between areas chosen for study. Your state Sunday school secretary will be glad to furnish copies of this study series outline.

2. Assemblies

At the two Convention-wide assemblies, Glorieta and Ridgecrest, the very best leadership of the denomination is available to help Sunday school teachers through group and individual conferences. At these assemblies year after year, hundreds of Intermediate workers receive a new understanding of responsibilities and new inspiration to try to do a better job.

Part of that inspiration comes through fellowship with other dedicated workers and through messages by inspired men of God, as well as through age-group conferences themselves.

The same benefits are also to be found in the assemblies sponsored by various states.

3. Clinics

Bible-teaching clinics on a state or regional level are another denominational aid to Sunday school teachers. Planned on a workshop basis, these clinics combine theory, practice, and inspiration, with the emphasis always on the practical aspects of teacher improvement.

Baptist state papers and denominational magazines announce dates of assemblies and clinics so that workers may avail themselves of these leadership training opportunities.

V. The Teacher's Counseling Role

As concepts of teaching have changed, the role of the teacher has also changed. Since his chief purpose is not to "impart knowledge," he is no longer just an instructor. Rather, he is the senior partner in the learning process, giving guidance to the pupil as he searches for help in making decisions. The Sunday school teacher is concerned primarily with helping his pupil find God's will in small matters as well as in large ones.

Adolescents do want help on questions of right and wrong, in distinguishing good and bad, but they will not accept help from a dictatorial Sunday school teacher, even though his intentions may be the very best.

So teachers are learning to *listen*, not just to talk. Instead of trying to make his pupils understand him and his point of view, the teacher's first concern is to understand his pupils. Furthermore, he must accept them and respect them even though he cannot approve of some of their attitudes and actions.

When a teacher understands and accepts his pupils, he will find a way to share his convictions without "preaching at them." He will find a way to set firm and reasonable limits for Christian youth without resorting to pious platitudes or to the role of a dictator.

VI. Emphasis on Group Dynamics

In business, politics, and education (including religious education), a great deal of emphasis is being put on group dynamics. A simple explanation of the term is this: group consideration and solution of a problem.

Business executives have learned that better ideas come from a session where ten salesmen think through and react to suggestions than from the executive director alone. A wise

Sunday school superintendent does not hand out to his workers tailor-made suggestions for carrying out a promotional job that must be done. Instead, he describes the problem and then lets the group of workers decide how they can best handle it.

This same principle of group dynamics works on a class level, too. Response will be much better if Intermediate boys decide what they want to do at Christmas time as an expression of their appreciation of God's love than if the teacher simply announces for all to bring canned goods to be carried to a needy family he has selected. Of course, the Intermediates will be led to keep their project in line with church policy.

The responsibility of a teacher who uses group dynamics is greater, not less, than that of teachers who do all the planning themselves. He is responsible for making *the group feel responsible* for achieving goals that are in keeping with the moral and spiritual values revealed in the Word of God. Yet he must do so in such a way that ideas will come from the group and will reflect actual group thinking—not skilful manipulation on his part.

VII. Evaluation of Teaching

It takes a certain amount of maturity for a teacher to be willing or able to evaluate his own work honestly or to invite another to evaluate it for him. Sunday schools do not have to undergo inspection, and teachers do not have to accept supervision. But the quality of teaching is being evaluated anyway.

1. *Pupil Reaction*

Not too long ago a group of high school students in Portsmouth, Virginia, began discussing Sunday school one day during a secular school class period. Because interest was so high, the teacher postponed the activity scheduled for the hour and listened as they revealed their dissatisfactions. This is his description of the class of thirty students, approximately fourteen years of age:

> Most members lived in suburban areas; they came from families in the middle-income or somewhat higher groups. A majority of the members were interested in social activities of many sorts, in some cases to the detriment of their academic activities. Most attended Sunday school and church fairly regularly; some held offices in Sunday school or young people's groups in church. Two or three were Catholic, and perhaps the same number had no religious affiliation to my knowledge; the majority were Protestants, of a variety of denominations. There did not seem to be any appreciable difference between the various religious groups concerning their attitudes about the failures of the Sunday school.

The following are this teacher's summary of the comments his students made in evaluating their Sunday school:

> Some Sunday schools are too passive; there is not enough active pupil participation.
> Some teachers are not prepared; presentations are often dull; there is not enough "meat" in lessons.
> There is a lack of variety of activities; there is a lack of organization of activities.
> In the church program, there is a lack of emphasis on church-sponsored teen-age recreation; facilities for recreation are often lacking or deficient.
> Emphasis in Sunday school is often on extraneous goals, such as the scoring of so many points or getting so many stars, rather than on spiritual growth.[4]

How would you react to such criticism if it had come directly from the Intermediates you teach? Though yours may not be so verbal as the Virginia group, you may be sure that they are evaluating the job you are doing. Evaluation, unfavorable criticism included, can be the basis for real growth if the teacher accepts it in the right spirit. Good teachers, and those who want to be good at the job, are concerned with pupil reaction.

2. *Knowledge Acquired*

This statement is true: "Knowledge tests memory; living tests learning." [5] Even so, knowledge tests are worthwhile because knowledge, when properly used, is an important aid to spiritual growth. Certainly it is not to be scorned, even though attitudes and conduct are of more significance. It is only when considered as an end in itself that knowledge is valued too highly.

So teachers should be interested in ascertaining what factual knowledge pupils have acquired. This kind of testing is quite possible, though not so simple if findings are to be scientifically accurate. True-false, multiple choice, and completion tests (well-known types) can, when carefully planned, prove to be valuable testing instruments in the knowledge area.

3. *Inward Changes*

"Living tests learning." The kind of living the Intermediates in your class are doing now and will do in the years ahead is the best evaluation of the quality of your teaching. That living must be measured through their sense of values as revealed in their attitudes and actions. How do they (and how will they) feel and think and act in regard to lost people? minority groups? money? marriage? politics?

Though it is not easy, it is possible to devise questions to be answered and problems to be solved which will indicate whether teachers are co-operating with pupils and the Holy Spirit in such a way as to bring about Christian growth. The attendance record, the effort of pupils to enlist others and to win the lost to Christ, life commitment to Christian service, tithing, and daily choices are tangible indications of whether teaching is affecting living in the right way.

This book opened with a verse of Scripture cautioning one not to accept a teaching responsibility lightly. Let it close with a prayer for wisdom and with a promise of power to one who believes:

> I never give up praying for you; and this is my prayer. That God, the God of our Lord Jesus Christ and the all-glorious Father, will give you spiritual wisdom and the insight to know more of Him: that you may receive that inner illumination of the spirit which will make you realize how great is the hope to which He is calling you—the magnificence and splendour of the inheritance promised to Christians—and how tremendous is the power available to us who believe in God (Eph. 1:16–20 Phillips).[6]

FOR FURTHER CONSIDERATION

1. Share with the group an account of some efforts you have made to enlist family co-operation.
2. (a) What other organizations in your church are working with teen-agers? Do you know their objectives?
   (b) What secular organizations of a character-building type are working with these same youngsters? What are their objectives?
3. What are the chief weaknesses of having someone teach the lesson every Wednesday night at the officers and teachers' meeting?
4. What are some basic counseling principles every Sunday school teacher should know and practice?

---

[1] H. H. Remmers and D. H. Radler, *The American Teenager* (Indianapolis: The Bobbs-Merrill Co., Inc., 1957), p. 250. Used by special permission of publishers.

[2] Ruth Strang, *The Adolescent Views Himself* (New York: McGraw-Hill Book Co., Inc., 1957), p. 361. Used by permission.

[3] *Ibid.*, p. 20. Used by permission.

[4] Fred Tubbs, "How Youth Feels About Sunday School," *Religious Herald*, Sept. 12, 1957. Used by permission.

[5] Nathaniel Freeman Cantor, *Teaching-Learning Process* (New York: The Dryden Press, 1953), p. 309. Used by permission of Henry Holt and Company, Inc.

[6] J. B. Phillips, *The New Testament in Modern English* (New York: The Macmillan Co., copyright 1958 by J. B. Phillips), p. 412. Used by permission.

Suggestions for the Teacher
Who Leads in the Study of This Book

You may assume that your class members have some felt need for becoming better teachers of Intermediates. But you need more than this general concept of their needs. If possible, observe your prospective study class members in action in classroom teaching prior to the beginning of the study course. Talk with members of the church staff or other leaders about the weaknesses they have discovered in the teaching of Intermediates. If the study class will include representatives of a number of churches, seek to learn all you can about Intermediate work in each church.

PURPOSE

At best you will lack the knowledge of particular needs on which to make your teaching purpose specific. You can gain insight by asking each class member, as he registers, to include on his slip answers to such questions as: In what department do you teach (if any)? What is the age range of your class? With what specific phases of teaching do you desire particular help— Bible using, pupil participation, lesson study, carry-over activities, or other matters?

As registrations are collected, glance rapidly at the responses to the last item and make mental notes about what your class members think are their greatest needs. (No answer or a very general answer will indicate that the individual probably does not know enough about good teaching techniques to be aware of specific needs.)

As later you give the registration slips concentrated study, you will list under your general aim specific needs of which your class members are already aware. You should also list needs of which you plan to make them become aware.

SUGGESTED ACTIVITIES

No person learns how to teach by hearing the leader of a study course lecture on teaching. Listening should be combined with various learning activities. In preparation for teaching this book you will wish to determine some activities you will suggest. Secure the materials needed and prepare such advance assignments as

125

should be made to insure effective use of these activities during the brief time available in class periods during the study course.

At the close of each chapter the author has included suggestions "For Further Consideration." Mark those you plan to use in class to "spark" meaningful discussion.

Plan to do together some of the activities suggested. See for example, page 23; suggestion 1 on page 85; suggestion 5 on page 94; suggestion 5 on page 109.

Note that some of the suggestions call for assignments and reports. See for example suggestions 1 and 4 on page 41; 2 on page 94; 1 on page 108.

Encourage each class member to head a page of his notebook: "What I Plan to Do." As he completes the study of a chapter, he should select one or two main ideas from that chapter that he will put into practice to improve his teaching. Department officers may list things they will help the teachers in their departments to do. Compiling these statements may be an activity for each individual, or it may become a group project.

You will wish to plan additional group activities, and to include others suggested by class members as the study progresses. For example—

Chapter 1.—In connection with suggestion 3 on page 9 lead the study group to examine the unit aim and the individual lesson aims for one quarter in one or more of the Intermediate lessons series being used by the departments represented. Ask class members in each case to decide which of the seven major objectives the lesson aim will help to reach.

Chapter 2.—Spend time on the project, suggested at the beginning of the study, of compiling statements about "What I Plan to Do." For chapter 1 these statements will deal with the improvement of use of teaching aims. For chapter 2, each worker should select three or four ways he will seek to improve himself as a worker.

Chapter 3.—Prior to the beginning of this study course, learn from the church librarian (in each church, if more than one is represented) what books on adolescents are available. Select some of these books (perhaps those named by the author on page 41) and assign in advance for brief reviews.

Lead each class member to examine the comments about pupil needs as found in the next four lessons in his teacher's book. Find evidence that these comments are in accord with the discussion of Intermediate characteristics in this chapter. (Let all workers who use the same lesson course group together for this activity.)

Chapter 4.—Ask each class member to recall and share with the group as many as possible of the questions Intermediates have asked him during the past month (or a longer period). To what extent do these questions indicate that the Intermediate is being stimulated to think about significant religious and social problems?

Chapter 5.—Using some future lesson (perhaps the one for next Sunday) lead the group to assemble working tools for study as mentioned on pages 57 to 63 (previous assignment needed). Have them take steps 1 to 4 in lesson planning (see pages 63–66). If not all use the same lesson, group them according to the lessons used. Let each group appoint a leader and carry out the planning activity suggested.

Chapter 6.—Continue the lesson planning activity. Help your members to consider possible methods which seem appropriate for use in the lesson under consideration and to discuss the probable effectiveness of each method.

Chapter 7.—Continue work on the lesson plans started during the preceding periods. Follow the instructions in chapter 7.

Chapter 8.—Lead class members to review the lesson planning done thus far. If none has been done, the class may begin now to plan next Sunday's lesson, applying what has been discussed in chapters 5, 6, 7 and 8.

Ask workers from one department represented in your class to tell what occurred in last Sunday's assembly (previous assignment needed). Lead the class to evaluate this assembly from the standpoint of how it helped to prepare pupils for the study of the lesson itself.

Chapter 9.—Ask class members: What plans have you made for regular evaluation of your work as a teacher?

Share the cumulated notes in the "What I Plan to Do" lists—which were suggested as a project to run during the entire study. Engage in a prayer of mutual commitment to carrying out these plans.

Some Audio-Visual Materials

In many cases filmstrips or motion pictures may be used as extracurricular material for research or to supplement and enrich the class discussions. Such materials should be scheduled at a time other than the seven and one-half hours of classwork. In some cases a filmstrip or motion picture may be used in a class period to introduce a study. For example, the filmstrip *The Christian Teacher* may be so used (in its entirety, or selected frames).

A filmstrip such as *Selecting Aims* may tie so closely with the textbook discussion, and be effective for use during the class period.

Some of the following items are better suited for use as extra-curricular sources than for classroom showing.

Chapter 1
    MOTION PICTURE: *A Job or a Calling*

Chapter 2
    FILMSTRIP: *The Christian Teacher*

Chapter 3
    FILMSTRIPS: *Similarities of Growth; Differences in Growth*
    MOTION PICTURE: *Vocational Choice: A Partnership*

Chapter 4
    FILMSTRIP: *Selecting Aims*

Chapter 5
    MOTION PICTURE: *Preparing to Teach*

Chapter 6
    FILMSTRIP: *Choosing Methods*

Chapter 7
    FILMSTRIP: *Planning a Lesson*

Chapter 8
    MOTION PICTURE: *Teaching the Word*

Chapter 9
    FILMSTRIPS: *How to Have a Weekly Officers and Teachers' Meeting; Principles of Sunday School Growth; Testing Results; "Church-Related Vocations Series"*
    MOTION PICTURE: *The Great Challenge*

(The last named filmstrip is available from the Cokesbury Book Store, Nashville, Tennessee.)

For Review and Written Work

CHAPTER 1

1. Write a brief paragraph explaining why teaching is such serious business.
2. What is the major difference between preaching and teaching?
3. Put into a summarizing statement the basic ideas incorporated in the word "teaching" as applied to Sunday school.
4. List in abbreviated form seven major objectives of Christian education.

CHAPTER 2

5. Name six qualities or characteristics teen-agers like for their teachers to have. Rank them in order of importance (according to your judgment).
6. What are some safeguards against disciplinary problems?
7. Name several avenues teachers should explore in an effort to understand their pupils. Point out the relative value of each.
8. Comment on the importance of this statement: We can follow a good example better than a good lecture.

CHAPTER 3

9. Name five problems of deep concern to most teen-agers.
10. What are five goals or developmental tasks which should be achieved during adolescence?
11. Why should parents and Sunday school teachers not be unduly alarmed when Intermediates question beliefs and practices they have heretofore taken for granted?

CHAPTER 4

12. What two factors are essential to learning?
13. Name five learning skills which nearly all Intermediates possess.
14. What kind of classroom situation is favorable to learning?

15. State four directives which, if followed, should result in effective teaching.

CHAPTER 5

16. Suggest several advantages in having a regular time and place for studying a Sunday school lesson.
17. In addition to current pupil and teacher periodicals, what other resource materials will teachers find helpful in preparing to teach?
18. Name five steps in lesson preparation.
19. What factors determine the learning goal (goals) in a given lesson?

CHAPTER 6

20. Give a simple definition of the term "teaching methods."
21. Name four factors to be considered in choosing a teaching method.
22. What is the chief weakness of lecturing?
23. Name at least five ways of teaching which appeal to teenagers. Which of these did you use last Sunday? Which have you never tried to use?
24. Describe several different ways to help pupils use their Bibles effectively in class.

CHAPTER 7

25. Name three major steps in a teaching plan.
26. Suggest several ways whereby a teacher may help create a favorable learning situation.
27. What is the relationship between the learning goal and the third step in the teaching plan?
28. What are the advantages of writing out a weekly teaching plan?

CHAPTER 8

29. Under what conditions is an opening assembly a learning opportunity of the right sort?
30. Recall the five steps in lesson preparation.
31. What is the learning goal for next Sunday's lesson as suggested in the teacher book? (Give the lesson date and title.)
32. Identify the method suggested in next Sunday's lesson for creating a learning situation.

33. What other methods were used in the remainder of the procedure suggested?

Chapter 9

34. Discuss some values of a well-planned parent-worker meeting.
35. What important opportunities does the weekly officers and teachers' meeting provide for the individual teacher?
36. What ways does a teacher have of knowing whether he **is** **doing** an acceptable job with his class?